SANTA
VS
SATAN

SANTA ★VS★ SATAN

THE OFFICIAL FIGHTS
COMPENDIUM OF IMAGINARY

★ JAKE KALISH ★

ILLUSTRATIONS BY CHRISTOPHER FROST

THREE RIVERS PRESS • NEW YORK

LIBRARY OF CONGRESS CATALOGING-IN-PUBLICATION DATA
KALISH, JAKE.
SANTA VS. SATAN : THE OFFICIAL COMPENDIUM OF IMAGINARY FIGHTS /
BY JAKE KALISH.—1ST ED.
1. HAND-TO-HAND FIGHTING—HUMOR.   I. TITLE.
PN6231.H33K35 2008
818'.602—DC22   2007046713

ISBN 978-0-307-40670-5

PRINTED IN THE UNITED STATES OF AMERICA

DESIGN BY MARIA ELIAS

10 9 8 7 6 5 4 3 2 1

FIRST EDITION

For all my vanquished foes
And for my folks, who knew not to ask what I was doing in my room

CONTENTS

FIGHTS FOR OUR WORLD

FIGHTS BECAUSE I SAID SO

SANTA
⋆VS⋆
SATAN

INTRODUCTION

Imaginary fights matter.

They always have and they always will. In the eighth century, the Norse hero Sigurd was summoned to slay the dragon Fafnir. Twelve hundred years later, little Sigurds all over the world kill dragons from their living rooms, with the power of their mighty dice. Lest you think fantasy battles these days are limited to board games played by dorky tweens, get into a discussion of faith sometime. Imaginary fights motivate myriad differences in religious belief: Jesus vs. Yahweh vs. Allah vs. Man. God vs. the Devil vs. little old you. And what'll happen when Christ comes down to separate the sinners from the saints? Judgment Day (No, I'm not talking *Terminator 2: Judgment Day*, although that's good too) is an imaginary fight of the utmost consequence, with awfully predictable winners. Now check out politics: The Cold War, which dominated the second half of the twentieth century, hinged on an imaginary fight—Who would win World War III? Could anyone? Often, the imaginary fights go far better than actual ones; the conflict in Iraq was supposed to be done in a couple of months and cost three billion dollars, with American soldiers embraced by freedom-loving arms. Years later, we can only imagine if Dungeon Master Cheney had been playing with dice instead of American lives. In the realm of pop culture, *Star Wars*, the most popular movie franchise of all time, gave us imaginary fights on two levels. While Jedi battled Sith with light sabers on Death Stars (Made up. Not real.), each fictional individual fought his own internal imaginary battle between the Force and the Dark Side.

The imaginary fight taps into the most primal part of the male psyche and imagination: the need to know who's the best, the strongest, the caveman with the biggest club. This need starts in infancy and never goes away; it lurks in the hearts of the most peaceful, benevolent men. Buddha occasionally strayed from the Noble Eightfold Path by wondering if he could take the Hindu Gods Vishnu and Shiva. There is no factual evidence for that, but it must be true. He couldn't possibly avoid it. He was still going to do his meditation thing, but whatever. This, the sad truth be told, is what guys care about. "Who would win between . . ." is one of man's three most fundamental questions, ahead of "Why are we here?" and behind "Who's hotter?" When Vern asked Teddy, "You think Mighty Mouse could beat up Superman?" in *Stand by Me,* we laughed, but not before we wondered.

I first wrote about imaginary fights in 2003 for *Playboy* magazine when the films *The Incredible Hulk* and *Terminator 3* were released. My assignment was the stuff of Woodward and Bernstein's dreams: Find who'd win a battle between the Hulk and the Terminator. No personal speculation allowed, experts were required to provide a definitive answer. I interviewed three men: Colonel Avery Chenoweth, a Marine combat artist and author of *Art of War;* Dr. Clark Hung, an associate professor of biomedical engineering at Columbia University; and Jim McLauchlin, then a contributing editor at *Wizard: The Comics Magazine,* now the editor-in-chief of Top Cow Productions. I wasn't worried about Captain Comics, but I was concerned the military expert and scientist would immediately dismiss me as frivolous and get back to their wars and atoms. On the contrary, Chenoweth and Hung were positively giddy to discuss the imaginary fight and approached the question with the depth of intelligence and logic they normally reserved for their "serious" concerns. (Recognizing, I like to believe, that nothing is more serious than an imaginary fight.) McLauchlin, the comics guy, was excited as well but had considered it all before. He, you see, was responsible each month for reading and answering letters from readers who just *had* to know the winners of fights between, say, Batman and Spider-Man, The Flash and Daredevil, the Silver Surfer and the Green Lantern. Jim McLauchlin is, no kidding, probably the world's foremost expert on imaginary fights between superheroes. And I can't imagine many better things to be. Ruler of the Heavens and Earth is good, but it's taken. In the end the score was Hulk: 2, Terminator: 1, with the biomedical engineer contending the Hulk "is governed by rage, making him more fallible."

Most freelance writers would consider themselves lucky if they got one imaginary fight assignment, but I've been blessed with two. Recently, *Men's Fitness* asked if I knew a "comic book expert" who could decide the winner of an NCAA-style tournament pitting superheroes against one another in imagined battles. Did I know an expert? I was soon talking to McLauchlin, but not before all my male friends from work strongly voiced their opinions, their excited comments often preceded by "Ooh! Ooh! Ooh!"—intelligent young professionals suddenly Arnold Horshacks on speed. Because imaginary fights mattered to them, far more than the mundane adult responsibilities upon which their livelihoods depended. I know what you're thinking: *But that's juvenile.* Yeah, and? So are we. *Maxim,* for which I've written dozens of articles, boasts over a million readers monthly, without a single article of or concerning sociopolitical impact. Every man hides an inner boy, and he usually doesn't hide him too well.

In writing the *Men's Fitness* tournament of superheroes article, it occurred to me that discussion of imaginary fights could not, should not, nay, *must* not be limited to the superhero realm, nor be constrained by the tiny boxing ring of a couple of articles. This means *far* too much, and these combatants fight on a battlefield bounded only by the imagination. Wondering about Michael Corleone vs. Tony Montana? Wonder no more. Considering the Lucky vs. the Skilled? I got you, kid. The imaginary fight envelops the world of ideas, wrapping its burly, bear-hugging arms around our collective consciousness. Or something like that. But dig it: What if, in lieu of debating the psychological ramifications of the virgin/whore dichotomy, we just had a virgin and a whore fight? Wouldn't that be better? Suppose, instead of pontificating on the cycle of life, we let the Stork and the Grim Reaper duke it out? Rather than evolutionary biologists and fundamentalist kooks getting into a dead-end argument over Intelligent Design, mightn't you prefer Charles Darwin and Adam squaring off? Perhaps all our questions could be answered. And maybe, just maybe, the world would be a simpler and better place. Imagine.

FIGHTS
FOR OUR LIVES

**BATTLES THAT DETERMINE THE
ULTIMATE MEANING OF OUR
INDIVIDUAL EXISTENCES**

THE ONE YOU LOVE

ALLY: You

ENEMY: You

TRADEMARK FIGHTING MOVE: The Unrequited Uppercut

CHARACTERISTICS: Beautiful and perfect

GLIMMER OF HOPE #1: You think you thought you saw her glance at you or at least near you with something that could be interpreted as desire one time when she was drunk.

GLIMMER OF HOPE #2: It all seemed so right when you made love in your dreams.

GLIMMER OF HOPE #3: She couldn't have said "stop looking at me" if she hadn't been looking too.

WHAT SHE MEANS BY "YOU'RE CREEPING ME OUT": Touch me.

AMBIGUOUS STATEMENT THAT MIGHT MEAN SHE LOVES YOU: "I think we should be friends."

WHY SHE TALKS ABOUT OTHER MEN SHE FINDS ATTRACTIVE: To make you jealous.

THE ONE YOU'RE WITH

ALLY: You

ENEMY: You

TRADEMARK FIGHTING MOVE: The Slam of Settling

NICKNAME: The Gravedigger of Dreams (it's a long nickname)

ANNOYING HABIT: Talking to you when you're not listening.

HER REASON TO DOUBT THE DEPTH OF YOUR LOVE: You said "me too" after sighing and before looking at your watch.

WHAT YOU TELL YOUR FRIENDS: "She's a good woman."

WHAT THAT MEANS: You're not sure.

MAJOR POINT IN HER FAVOR #1: She's right there.

MAJOR POINT IN HER FAVOR #2: She makes a mean lasagna.

MAJOR POINT IN HER FAVOR #3: She said she'd try to lose weight.

MAJOR PROBLEM: She takes up a significant portion of your queen-sized bed.

THE ONE YOU LOVE

SUPERPOWER: She makes you willing to sell out anyone and anything.

WHY YOU'RE BETTER THAN THE RICHER, BETTER-LOOKING, MORE CONFIDENT AND MATURE MAN SHE'S WITH: Because you're you.

RUMOR ABOUT HER YOU TRIED TO START WHEN SHE DIDN'T RESPOND TO YOUR DRUNKEN PHONE CALLS AND E-MAILS: She has genital warts.

SOUL-CRUSHING TACTIC: She once tried to hook you up with her ugly friend.

HOW GOOD YOU IMAGINE SHE'D BE IN BED, ON A SCALE OF ONE TO TEN: Eleven

HOW GOOD YOU IMAGINE YOU'D BE IN BED WITH HER, ON A SCALE OF ONE TO TEN: Thirteen

ONLY REASON TO DOUBT HER BRILLIANCE: That she fails to recognize yours.

THE ONE YOU'RE WITH

WHAT YOU DO AFTER SHE GOES TO BED EARLY AND YOU KISS HER GOODNIGHT ON THE FOREHEAD: Masturbate with unbelievable vigor to increasingly disturbing pornography.

WHAT JUST HAPPENED: She said something really important you didn't hear and wouldn't have understood anyway.

WHAT SHE TELLS HER FRIENDS: You're much better in private.

IS THAT TRUE?: She hopes one day it will be.

THINGS SHE FEIGNS INTEREST IN TO KEEP CONVERSATIONS GOING: Your favorite sports teams; your least favorite gastrointestinal ailments

THINGS YOU FEIGN INTEREST IN TO KEEP CONVERSATIONS GOING: Antiquing; kittens; foliage

EXPERT ANALYSIS

"The one you love has obvious physical advantages, being faster and harder and unlike the one you're with, unburdened by the time-consuming mercy that comes from being a nice person. Indeed, the one you love is a wickedly aggressive foe, not afraid to fight dirty and break any, if not all, rules. However, the one you're with has super manipulative strategic abilities that come from practicing on you but also from being substantially less moronic than the one you love. The one you're with also has the fine-tuned power to be both numb and deaf at will, which in a fight against a crazy, albeit hot, sex machine would ultimately create an insurmountable advantage, especially if anything negative happened in the universe, like a professional rejection or flu...either of which would send the one you love running."

—Tanya Allen, actress,
Silent Hill, Starhunter,
The Newsroom, Regeneration

"The one you love often sends wistful e-mails with impeccable spelling and poignantly apropos literary references, but the one you're with usually has an enormous cock. (There's a reason, you know). The one you're with wins. You spend the rest of your life feeling bad about the one you love."

—Jennifer Dziura, comedian, blogger
(www.jenisfamous.com)

"The one you're with is tired, fatigued, and old—which is why you're in love with someone else to start with. Don't be fooled, though: There's no wife on Earth who's ever too tired to take you for every penny you've got, as well as your home, car, kids, and cat, just as soon as she finds out about the one you love! She may be so tired (of you) that she should theoretically come last (if she can be bothered to come at all with you in her bed), but you can bet that she'll be through those courtroom doors like a ferret down a drainpipe. The one you're with wins every time. No contest, fellas."

—Kathleen Charlotte, author,
Va-Va-Voodoo!: Find Love,
Make Love & Keep Love

THE FIGHT

The One You Love immediately beats the One You're With to within an inch of her life, but then starts making out with the referee and leaves with him before the fight is over. Judges are forced to award the match to the gnarled, broken One You're With, who celebrates by crying herself to sleep.

THE WINNER

THE ONE YOU'RE WITH (DQ)

THE BIGGEST MISTAKE OF YOUR LIFE BRAWL

BILL BUCKNER

vs.

THE BASEBALL THAT WENT BETWEEN HIS LEGS

BILL BUCKNER

ALLIES: His family; Mets fans

ENEMIES: Red Sox fans, especially before 2004

CAREER HITS: 2,715

BATTING TITLE: In 1980

RBI IN 1986: 102

HOW MUCH THE PREVIOUS THREE THINGS MATTER NOW: Not at all

WHAT HE'D DO DIFFERENTLY: Perhaps become a monk, or something else where no one notices when you fuck up.

WHERE HE MOVED AFTER RETIRING: Boise, Idaho, far away from major-league baseball

HOW HIS WHIFF ON MOOKIE WILSON'S SLOW-ROLLING GROUND BALL COMPARES WITH THE BIGGEST MISTAKE OF YOUR LIFE: It's exactly the same, except the whole world saw, it broke the heart of a city, and made his name synonymous with choking.

WHY IT WASN'T HIS FAULT #1: Calvin Schiraldi gave up three straight singles in that ninth inning.

THE BASEBALL THAT RUINED BUCKNER'S LIFE

ALLY: The baseball Steve Bartman interfered with

ENEMIES: People who find three-hour-plus baseball games deadly boring

SIZE: 9 inches in circumference

WEIGHT: 5 ounces

STITCHES: 108

CONTROVERSIAL PERIOD FOR HIS YOUNGER BROTHERS: The late '90s, when the balls were as juiced as the players.

WHERE HE WOUND UP: First was bought by Charlie Sheen, now in the collection of some guy named Seth Swirsky.

RECURRING NIGHTMARE: That he was fielded cleanly by Buckner and tossed away by an umpire without ever getting to go on the celebrity circuit and pick up hot young female baseballs.

WHAT HE'D DO DIFFERENTLY: Not a goddamned thing—he's famous.

BILL BUCKNER

WHY IT WASN'T HIS FAULT #2: Bob Stanley threw a wild pitch to tie up the game.

WHY IT WASN'T HIS FAULT #3: Red Sox manager John McNamara not only didn't pinch-hit Don Baylor for Buckner in the eighth inning, he didn't replace Buckner in the tenth with Dave Stapleton, a far better glove man who had served as a late-inning defensive replacement for Buckner in all of Boston's playoff wins that year.

HOW GRATEFUL SCHIRALDI, STANLEY, AND MCNAMARA ARE THAT ONLY DORKY BASEBALL NERDS REMEMBER HOW BAD THEY WERE BECAUSE BUCKNER SCREWED UP A PLAY A LITTLE LEAGUER COULD HAVE MADE: Extremely

REASON TO FORGIVE BUCKNER, BESIDES THE FACT IT'S WHAT JESUS WOULD DO: He's gone to various functions with Mookie Wilson over the years, and signed "oops" on pictures of him chasing after the ball that went through his legs. Really.

THE FIGHT

Bill Buckner discovers a time machine on his property that takes him back to October 25, 1986. Mookie's ground ball rolls toward him, and this time he's ready, in perfect fielding position, to recapture his good name when the baseball bounces up and hits him squarely in the head, killing him instantly. He spends all of eternity repeatedly trying to field a ball slowly rolling toward him. It never goes well.

THE WINNER

THE EVIL BASEBALL (KO)

ADAM

CREATED: In God's image

APPEARANCE: Godlike

ANCESTRY: The first man created by the Almighty One

BACKGROUND: Immortality

DOMINION: Over every creeping thing that creepeth upon the earth, except the gay things, which sashayeth

LIFE SPAN: 930 years, which means a fortune in Social Security

ALLY: God, before he screwed that sweet deal up

ENEMIES: Talking snake; pushy woman; God after all that schmucky apple business

TASK: Just had to do nothing, and couldn't

TRADEMARK FIGHTING MOVE: The Paradise Pile Driver

EVIDENCE OF INTELLIGENT DESIGN: Babies and rainbows

BIBLE PARADOX: If God is omnipotent, how can man have free will?

CHARLES DARWIN

CREATED: By monkeys, through magic

APPEARANCE: Apelike

ANCESTRY: Descended from monkeys, namely his parents, Bubbles and Koko Darwin

BACKGROUND: Geology

FUN FACT: Currently a resident of Hell, where he will be sodomized by apes for eternity

LIFE SPAN: 73 years

ALLIES: Doomed, godless "scientists"; "people with a proper education"

ENEMIES: The Religious Right; God

TRADEMARK FIGHTING MOVE: The Flying Elbow of Evolution

EVIDENCE OF EVOLUTION: God sure didn't make yo mama.

EVOLUTION PARADOX: If we're descended from monkeys, how come we can't swing on trees? Because that would be cool.

ADAM

HIS FUNDAMENTAL RELIGIOUS QUESTION: How come that stupid snake had to open its goddamned mouth?

SCUZZY INTERPRETATION OF HIS TEXT: It's Adam and Eve, not Adam and Steve.

KEY TO SURVIVAL OF SPECIES: Not pissing God off

COOL BOB DYLAN SONG: "The Gates of Eden"

WHAT HE ART: Dust

SEMINAL WORK: The Fall of Man

INFLUENTIAL VOYAGE: Out of Paradise, to the cursed ground

WACKY IRONY: In "Paradise," the only woman is your sister, and you can't get a damn pair of pants.

CHARLES DARWIN

HIS FUNDAMENTAL RELIGIOUS QUESTIONS: How could a beneficent God allow a child to die? Also, if we're descended from God and not monkeys, how come I love throwing my feces so much?

SCUZZY INTERPRETATION OF HIS TEXT: Eugenics

KEY TO SURVIVAL OF SPECIES: The natural selection of advantageous traits

COOL BOB DYLAN SONG: The unreleased "Mr. Tambourine Monkey"

WHAT HE ART: A chimp with a pen

SEMINAL WORK: *The Origin of Species*

INFLUENTIAL VOYAGE: Through the Galápagos Islands on the HMS *Beagle*

WACKY IRONY: Late in life, with that big white beard, Darwin kind of looked like God.

EXPERT ANALYSIS

Declined to comment: God

"Darwin lived to be 73, and he was an invalid for much of his adult life, while Adam lived to be 930, and presumably was doddering in his last few centuries. But it's only fair to compare them when they were in their prime: in Darwin's case, when he was between college and the voyage of the *Beagle;* in Adam's case, when he was still in the Garden of Eden, before his rib was removed. It seems clear that Darwin would have won their fight then. He was fond of shooting, whereas Adam, as the first man, was obviously inexperienced and unsophisticated with any sort of weaponry, or even with fisticuffs. And as the proverb goes, you should never, ever, bring a naif to a gunfight."

—Glenn Branch, deputy director,
National Center for Science Education
(www.ncseweb.org)

"I believe the fight involving Adam vs. Charles Darwin is not representative of Darwin's actual challenge. The better fight is: 'Behe vs. Darwin.' (Author's note: Michael Behe is a prominent intelligent design advocate and author.) Behe will win because the mechanism postulated by Darwin, random variation acted on by environmental sorting, lacks the capacity to generate the biological information necessary to produce, operate, and maintain living systems."

—John Calvert, managing director,
Intelligent Design Network
(www.intelligentdesignnetwork.org)

"The fight starts with Adam kicking Darwin, sending the father of natural selection tumbling in the dust. In severe pain, Darwin feels the ground for anything he might use in his defense. He finds a rib and when Adam pounces on him, Darwin jabs Adam in the eye. Blood gushes forth upon the ground from Adam's eye socket. In agony, he slips on his own blood and falls next to Darwin, who is still holding the rib. He looks at Darwin through his one good eye and says: 'I've got God on my side. I can't lose.' Darwin stands up, brushes himself off, and tosses the rib at Adam's side. 'And I've got evidence on my side.' Darwin walks away, hears a hissing sound, smiles, and declares that it was a good day, though too long in coming."

—Robert Todd Carroll, author,
The Skeptic's Dictionary
(www.skepdic.com)

"Adam would beat Darwin—because, as the collective abilities of the human species (combined with technology) increase over the long term, so our individual, personal capabilities decline. Adam must have been the greatest ever human, since he had to do everything that needed to be done, and clearly did it well enough to enjoy unparalleled reproductive success. (I'm assuming that there were other Adams around at the time, whom he outcompeted—and who notably failed to win Eve's favor.)"

—Bruce Charlton, editor of *Medical Hypotheses* magazine, author of *The Modernization Imperative,* and champion of the theory of psychological neoteny, which states that it is advantageous in both science and modern life to have a personality type characterized by prolonged youthfulness

"It's very simple and logical. Adam can never win. It's the basic theory of Lovism: The only powers left to a man after he says, 'I love you,' are the powers to take out the garbage. Fighting is for the single."

—Keith and the Girl, hosts of the free comedy show and podcast found at www.keithandthegirl.com

"A quick fight. When Adam drops his fig leaf to strike, Charles Darwin, a proper Victorian gentleman of notoriously poor health, will die of shame."

—Matthew Polly, author, *American Shaolin: Flying Kicks, Buddhist Monks, and the Legend of Iron Crotch*

THE FIGHT

A tanned, buff Darwin, who has been training with his ape brothers, is ready for combat, but Adam is a no-show, and the judges are beginning to suspect he may just be a metaphor for humanity. Then, by intelligent design, the first man appears out of nowhere, accompanied by his promoter, an evil snake. The snake hands Darwin a copy of Michael Behe's *The Edge of Evolution: The Search for the Limits of Darwinism.* Darwin is fascinated to discover what a naive dope he is, and becomes so engrossed in the book he doesn't notice God rearing back to kick him in the balls.

THE WINNER

ADAM (KO)

SANTA

ORIGIN: Variation of a Dutch fairy tale based on St. Nicholas, a bishop from the former Asia Minor who helped the needy and suffering by getting them PS3s

ALIASES: Father Christmas; Kris Kringle; Saint Nick

OCCUPATION: Brings toys to all good little boys and girls, so long as they're Gentiles

RESIDENCE: In the North Pole; in the hearts of Gentile children everywhere

ALSO FOUND IN: Department stores

ALLIES: Reindeer; Mrs. Claus; anybody selling anything

ENEMIES: Those who don't believe in magic and wonder and joy

DEFENDERS: Stress the importance of lying to kids early.

VALUE TO CHILDREN: Gives them hope, makes them behave.

DOES HE EXIST?: Yes, Virginia.

SATAN

ORIGIN: Fallen angel, like Dana Plato

ALIASES: The Devil; The Antichrist; Beelzebub; Lord of the Flies; Mephistopheles, The Blasphemer; Prince of Darkness; El Diablo; His Infernal Majesty; like a thousand other things you could totally name your rock band

OCCUPATION: Ruler of the Underworld; Marlboro ad exec in charge of youth marketing

RESIDENCE: Hell

ALSO FOUND IN: Your evil heart

ALLIES: Hitler; Stalin; that bartender who cut you off when you weren't even really drunk

ENEMIES: The Righteous

DEFENDERS: Say that without evil there can be no good.

VALUE TO CHILDREN: Scares the crap out of them, makes them behave.

DOES HE EXIST?: You'll find out if you keep masturbating.

SANTA

CRITICIZED FOR: The commercialization of Jesus' birthday; revealing humanity's irrepressible greed

BIBLICAL REFERENCE: Luke 4:50 — "He who behaveth like a good little boy shall receive an action figure of the Spider-Man."

SONGS: The extremely corny "Here Comes Santa Claus"; "Santa Claus Is Coming to Town"

VEHICLE: Reindeer-powered sleigh

NOT RECOGNIZED BY: Non-Christians and other assholes

CONSPIRATORIAL CLAIM: That Santa is a hidden representation of Satan, with their being anagrams

TROUBLING QUESTION #1: Why does he give the most to those who need it the least?

TROUBLING QUESTION #2: Where does he park the reindeer?

FOLLOWERS: Hang out in shopping malls.

SATAN

CRITICIZED FOR: Relaxing strict residency requirements in Hell for atheists, gays

BIBLICAL REFERENCE: Ephesians 2:2 — "the spirit that now worketh in the children of disobedience."

SONGS: The completely awesome "Sympathy for the Devil"; "Hell's Bells"; "Highway to Hell"; "Hellhound on My Trail"; "Running with the Devil"; "Way Down in the Hole"; and even "Hell Is for Children" if no one is around to make fun of you.

VEHICLE: SUV

NOT RECOGNIZED BY: Folks who don't mind an eternity of hellfire

CONSPIRATORIAL CLAIM: That he only exists to sell Judas Priest and Marilyn Manson records

TROUBLING QUESTION #1: Does he exist independently of God?

TROUBLING QUESTION #2: If Heaven is supposed to be so great, why does Hell get the people who throw the best parties?

FOLLOWERS: Hang out in shopping malls.

EXPERT ANALYSIS

"My sensible money's on Satan. He's the Dark Prince, the Father of Lies, the Lord of the Underworld. He has plagues, demonic hordes of the damned, and the power of Temptation itself at his disposal. Santa Claus is, in the final analysis, just Santa. He knows if you've been bad or good, though his ability to do anything with that information seems limited. So it's a foregone conclusion—Old Nick beats Saint Nick. But secretly I'm rooting for Santa Claus."

—Dale Dobson, humorist for *Cracked, National Lampoon,* and *Yankee Pot Roast*

"One would think that Satan would have a clear advantage in this battle, what with the eternal fires of hell in his grasp, but you can't count out Santa. This is a man who has lived for thousands of years on a steady diet of rancid milk and stale cookies, yet he's still able to muster the strength to soar through the air in the middle of a cold winter night. So what if the two decided to go head to head? Didn't you ever hear that song about how Santa's "gonna find out who's naughty or nice"? Well, who's naughtier than Satan? Santa won't give him coal, he'll give him an ass-whuppin' instead. Beelzebub may be a beefcake for all I know, but Santa has the belly of a Sumo and that's just not something the prince of darkness is prepared

to tango with. Santa would eat him for breakfast, crap him out, wrap the remains in a gift box and give them to some unfortunate kid who was 'naughty' to teach him a lesson. Ho, ho, ho!"

—Roger Barr, www.i-mockery.com

"My first instinct is to vote for the horned wonder. He's been doling out beatings since before mankind roamed this ball of dirt. Moreover, if Santa has any notions of this being a fair fight, you would think the devil, who is not constrained by such petty concerns, would have it in the bag. However, one cannot overlook the advantage of Santa's Elves. These crafty little bastards are industrious, and have no qualms about being dishonest. After all, they stamp 'Made in China' on most of the toys they make ... You may think that's a minor point, but think of all the headaches it caused for Mattel. How many of those 'Chinese' toys made with lead-based paint actually came out of Santa's workshop? Seems like the fat man and his diminutive crew are taking a hardline against bad kids ...

"Sure, Satan has the damned on his side, but can a few Enron executives really stack up against the genius behind the largest toy recall in history? The only thing I can say with any degree of certainty is that the winner of this match will be wearing a red suit and will have a very annoying laugh. Talk to your bookie and see what the odds are. If they're in favor of Satan, bet on Santa and look for Satan to take a dive and collect his winnings."

—Ben Schulz, Satanist and webmaster of www.devilzown.com

"Satan—known as the Prince of Darkness and Lord of this world—might be assumed to have the edge in a physical encounter. The fallen, but formerly most beautiful, angel who was second only to his supposed creator would be expected to wield powers far greater than a pudgy elderly fellow who hobnobs with toy making little folk and flying reindeer. Having been the commander of legions of rebel angels, "The Man Downstairs" would be expected to have more experience in combat situations. Of course, if the conflict were sumo-styled and both were considered to be roughly the same height, the northern chap might have a weight advantage that could turn the tide in his favor."

—Peter H. Gilmore, high priest, Church of Satan (www.churchofsatan.com)

THE FIGHT

While Santa knows when you've been sleeping and knows when you're awake, Satan knows you'll fucking kill if it means you'll get what you want. So he enlists an army of children disappointed with their Christmas presents, promising them all they'll get a gift they'll never forget if they help him defeat Father Christmas. Millions of little warriors rip off Santa's limbs and feed them to him, and don't even ask what happens to the helpers and reindeer. Satan gives all the kids herpes and condemns them to Hell.

THE WINNER

SATAN (KO)

THE LUCKY

ALIASES: Lucky SOB; Lucky Cocksucker; Idiot Who's Too Stupid to Know How Fucking Lucky He Is; The Man

SUPERPOWER: Ability to fall headfirst into cash, sex, power while the smarter and more talented struggle against obstacle after obstacle

OCCUPATIONS: CEO of Daddy's company; Money Magnet

DANGER: Can have you fired, killed.

ALLY: God, who apparently is a bit of an asshole himself

ENEMIES: The Skilled

HOBBIES: Wiping himself with $100 bills; bathing in liquid gold

WHAT HE FINDS FUNNY: Probability, reason, justice

RATIONALIST'S PERSPECTIVE: Luck is a logical fallacy completely explained by probability theory. And then a piano fell on his head.

CHARACTERISTICS: Silver spoon in mouth; world in the palm of his hand; head in ass

THE SKILLED

ALIASES: Guy Who Thought His Graduate Degree Was Worth Something; Genius of the Unemployment Line

SUPERPOWER: Ability to fail despite overwhelming preparedness for success

OCCUPATION: What does it matter? Nobody cares.

DANGER: May kill himself in a spectacular manner just so his obit in the paper contains the word "brilliant."

ALLIES: Other guys who deserve greatness but would settle for a little mediocrity.

ENEMIES: Bosses who don't appreciate him; women who don't understand him.

COMFORT: Will be famous posthumously like Kafka or Van Gogh—or at least that's what he tells himself.

HOBBY: Bringing up his SAT scores to strangers in cafés.

WHAT HE FINDS FUNNY: When stupid people fail, lucky people die.

CHARACTERISTICS: Complete inability to ignore or tolerate grammatical errors

THE LUCKY

CARTOON CHARACTER:
The Roadrunner

GODDESS: Fortuna

LOVE INTEREST: The Girl You Deserve

QUOTES: "Luck is the residue of design" and "Luck is what happens when preparation meets opportunity" — the offensively smug Branch Rickey and Seneca, respectively, both of whom died by being castrated and eaten alive by panthers.

IDOL: George W. Bush

RESIDENCES: Penthouse apartment; private island; White House (2000–2008)

BATTLE EXPERIENCE: Gets medical exemptions from wars for having a left leg a quarter inch shorter than the right and a lazy eye; spends wars in a cabana by the beach in Costa Rica, doing blow off a gorgeous native girl's breasts while his stocks quintuple

STRENGTH: Unbreakable

WEAKNESS: Eventually his luck will run out. Right?

TRADEMARK FIGHTING MOVES: The Fist of Fortune; The Knee of Nepotism

THE SKILLED

CARTOON CHARACTER:
Wile E. Coyote

GODDESS: Minnie Driver's character in *Good Will Hunting*

LOVE INTEREST: Would have one in a just world.

QUOTE: "You're a genius." —Mom

IDOLS: Albert Einstein; Leonardo da Vinci; that sophomore-year philosophy professor who, rumor has it, boned the super hot girl in the first row on multiple occasions

RESIDENCES: Parents' basement; friends' couches

BATTLE EXPERIENCE: Once expertly fought against the inanity of his company's sales plan, offering a brilliant and far more cost-effective alternative in a tour-de-force presentation to his boss, who stole his ideas and fired him for being a smart-ass.

STRENGTHS: Knowledge; aptitude

WEAKNESSES: Hair-trigger despondence; ennui

TRADEMARK FIGHTING MOVE: The Graduate Degree Dropkick

EXPERT ANALYSIS

"I'd have to think the Lucky would have no hope; they would stand around waiting for some drastic change in the weather that disorients the Skilled, or maybe a pebble that falls from a mountaintop that bonks the Skilled on the head. But luck is the residue of design . . . and the only residue we'll see here is blood from the Lucky's nose."

—Will Leitch, editor, Deadspin (www.deadspin.com)

"Lucky wins the first round, luckily enough, but Skilled figures things out quickly and, knowing he could easily knock Lucky out, goes nine more rounds just to prolong the pain. (The skills on this guy . . .) Unfortunately, shortly after, Skilled falls off a cliff and dies."

—Keith and the Girl, hosts of the free comedy show and podcast found at www.keithandthegirl.com

"The Lucky vs. the Skilled is at first glance just a spat like any other. On closer inspection, however, it is revealed to be the possible single greatest contributor to evolution as we know it.

"Luck is a spunky, highly entertaining fighter. Her style is as cocky as one is likely to see. Her punches lack a certain sting but usually they are many in number and more often than not, they tire poor Skill out. Skill's fierce concentration can often make him rather boring, even upsetting to watch, and consequently he is not likely to be the audience favorite. His brow is in a constant unattractive furrow while he keeps his feet firmly planted to time his swings and use his body weight with intelligence and care. Usually Luck manages to avoid these blows, in the magical way that only Luck can, but when a skilled hit does happen to land on Luck—who has so little experience with suffering—she can be killed in an instant! In the end, the fact that good luck can happen for the Skilled but skill cannot be chanced upon by the Lucky, leaves Skill with a small but heartwarming advantage in a universe of otherwise random doom and glory."

—Tanya Allen, actress, *Silent Hill, Starhunter, The Newsroom, Regeneration*

"As a believer in the maxim that it is better to be lucky than good, I predict that the Lucky will win by forfeit after the Skilled injures himself in training camp."

—Matthew Polly, author, *American Shaolin: Flying Kicks, Buddhist Monks, and the Legend of Iron Crotch*

THE FIGHT

The Skilled, with extensive Navy SEAL sniper training, has the Lucky targeted from five hundred yards away and is about to fire the single, fatal shot when a grand piano falls out of the sky, killing him instantly.

THE WINNER

LUCKY (TKO, PIANO)

MY DAD

HOBBY: Wrestling lions

GREAT MILITARY MOMENT: Gunned down thirty-two Vietcong while blinded by mustard gas.

ALLIES: Fellow Medal of Honor recipients

ENEMIES: Fear him

PHOTOS IN WALLET: All the children he's saved from burning buildings

IN WATER: Swam the English Channel.

IN THE AIR: Is a fighter pilot with more kills than the Red Baron.

FIGHTING RECORD: 137–0–1, one disputed tie with Bruce Lee

TRADEMARK FIGHTING MOVE: The Chi, or Fist of Death

NOSE: Broken nine times

HAIR: Crew cut, for his fallen brothers

DRINK: Bourbon, neat

YOUR DAD

HOBBIES: Collecting his breast milk; crocheting; making homemade greeting cards

GREAT MILITARY MOMENT: Won once in War when his 7 beat your mom's 6.

ALLIES: Fellow members of Oprah's Book-of-the-Month Club

ENEMIES: There are no bad people, just bad decisions.

PHOTOS IN WALLET: Other people's puppies and kittens

IN WATER: Wears a life preserver in the bath.

IN THE AIR: Takes Klonopin to sleep, but makes sure to tell the flight attendants to give him the free pretzels anyway.

FIGHTING RECORD: 0–7, with losses to Girl Scouts, nuns, and pacifists

TRADEMARK FIGHTING MOVE: The Shhh, or silent treatment

NOSE: Got it fixed to look just like Liz Taylor's.

MY DAD

FIGHTING STRATEGY: Disarm opponent in the quickest and most efficient manner possible

SPORTS: Has a 100-mph fastball; can reverse dunk; runs the 40 in 4 seconds flat.

NICKNAME: Captain

WEDNESDAY-NIGHT ACTIVITY: High-stakes poker

VEHICLE: Harley

INSTINCT: Killer

DRAWS: His gun

YOUR DAD

HAIR: The Rachel, for his favorite Friend, Jennifer Aniston

DRINK: Shirley Temple, with extra umbrellas

FIGHTING STRATEGY: Start to cry, hope for pity

SPORTS: He plays sometimes, but doesn't keep score.

NICKNAME: Girlfriend

WEDNESDAY-NIGHT ACTIVITY: Stitching and bitching

VEHICLE: Tricycle

INSTINCT: Maternal

DRAWS: Unicorns

EXPERT ANALYSIS

"This altercation is an excellent ex-ample of how one's ability to sustain harmony creates success in life. Jake Kalish's Dad is a compassionate and skilled warrior. He moves from cen-ter and understands that true power is generated from within. Your Dad is imbalanced, ego-driven, and contami-nated by negative emotions. Because his core is weak, his attacks are pow-erless and self-defeating. Jake Kalish's Dad remains calm, pauses, assesses the threat, and takes action efficiently, functionally, and victoriously. He is clearly the master of his own fate and the winner of this fight."

—Joseph Cardillo, martial arts master, author of *Bow to Life: 365 Secrets from the Martial Arts for Daily Life* and *Be Like Water: Practical Wisdom from the Martial Arts*

"Please, God, don't make me kill again."

—Howard Kalish, My Dad

THE FIGHT

Going into battle determined and stoic, My Dad is unnerved by Your Dad hug-ging him, crying, and handing him a poem about friendship. My Dad calmly explains they have to fight, and Your Dad begins scratching and swinging his handbag. My Dad grabs Your Dad by the scrunchie in his ponytail and flings him across the room. Fearing he may have killed Your Dad, My Dad walks over to the frail, sad little man, who grabs My Dad's balls and squeezes. This dirty move is completely ineffective, as My Dad has what the Spanish call *juevos de piedra* (testicles of stone). Though he had previously intended to be mer-ciful, my irritated father punches your shameful father, breaking his face in fifty places. Feeling guilty, My Dad pays for Your Dad's cosmetic surgery, which allows him to finally fulfill his dream of looking like Joy Behar. He loves it! Your Dad bakes My Dad cook-ies, and a friendship is born.

THE WINNER

MY DAD (KO)

THE VIRGIN

ALIAS: Mother Teresa; Britney Spears ca. 1999

OCCUPATION: Nun; Christian Rock enthusiast

ALLIES: Jesus; Allah; Yahweh; parents

ENEMIES: Horny men; fallen women

CHARACTERISTICS: Tightness with the Lord and of the poonanny

SUPERPOWERS: If attractive, can make man fight his true nature.

IDOL: Mother Mary, who was without sin

RELATIONSHIP TO THE LORD: Pray to him while on knees

IN TWENTY YEARS: Wife; mother

MUST-HAVE ACCESSORIES: Chastity belt; Bible

UNFORTUNATE BUT NECESSARY HYPOCRISY: Male virgins go by "dork" or "loser."

THE WHORE

ALIAS: Jenna Jameson; Britney Spears ca. right about now

OCCUPATION: Whore

ALLIES: All men who are not their fathers or brothers

ENEMIES: God; bitches who can't keep their men

CHARACTERISTICS: Loose morals; chocha

SUPERPOWERS: If good, can put legs behind head, fit entire penis into throat.

IDOL: Lindsay Lohan, who is without panties

RELATIONSHIP TO THE LORD: Call to him while on back

IN TWENTY YEARS: Whore with lower prices, standards

MUST-HAVE ACCESSORIES: Vibrator; herpes medicine

UNFORTUNATE BUT NECESSARY HYPOCRISY: Male whores go by "stud," "playa."

PARADOXICAL SUBGROUP: Born-again virgins

THE VIRGIN

PARADOXICAL SUBGROUP: The sexy "virgin whore," as exemplified by a young Jessica Simpson, Shiloh Jolie-Pitt*

THANKFUL FOR: The miracle of Immaculate Conception

AFTERLIFE: Hopefully much more exciting than actual life

PUNISHMENT ON EARTH: Never know the joy of a good deep dicking.

SEX APPEAL: Man wants what he cannot have.

BATTLE EXPERIENCE: Often fights her base desires, an immoral society.

SECRET WEAPON: God is on her side.

THE WHORE

THANKFUL FOR: The miracle of the morning-after pill

AFTERLIFE: Eternal hellfire

PUNISHMENT ON EARTH: Die first in horror movies, unless there's a black guy.

SEX APPEAL: Man wants what he can have.

BATTLE EXPERIENCE: Sometimes must fight pimp; bitches who can't keep their men

SECRET WEAPON: Platform heels are excellent for pussy-kicking

EXPERT ANALYSIS

"The Virgin would win for sure. She'd have to be strong. It takes way more strength to keep legs together than apart."

—Dr. Brian Parker, clinical sexologist, professor of human sexuality, sex expert for www.foreverpleasure.com

"Virgin may be bursting with untapped sexual energy that bodes well for fisticuffs, but all those years of repression make for passive-aggressive,

*Editor's note: Obviously, it is profoundly inappropriate to call a toddler a "virgin whore." Three Rivers Press offers its sincerest apologies. The authorities have been notified and Mr. Kalish's computer has been seized.

timid moves. Whore, on the other hand, works hard for her money. Her fuck-me heels and lady-of-the-night talons cut quite a swath across Virgin's prissy features. Not to mention all the dom moves she's mastered already in the bedroom. Winner: Whore."

—Lisa Rosman, film reviewer, blogger, The Broad View (http://lisarosman.blogspot.com)

"The Whore wins hands down (hands down being a place which, by definition, a virgin's never been). If you watch the great fights it's all about the leg movement. A virgin can't even pry hers apart."

—Kathleen Charlotte, author of Va-Va-Voodoo!: Find Love, Make Love & Keep Love

"The Whore wins. She isn't afraid to hike up her skirt and give it all she's got, while a virgin is afraid she'll get blood on her clothes. A virgin has all sorts of moral issues holding her back mentally, while a whore will do whatever it takes to get the job done and win."

—Donna Spangler, former Playboy model, author of How to Get a Rich Man

"The Whore would win the fight because she's streetwise and doesn't mind getting dirty. She may not be able to run too fast, but her shoes can be used as weapons. The Virgin can't do complicated fighting moves because she's afraid of breaking her hymen."

—editors, $pread: The Magazine by and for Sex Workers

"Well, you know the joke, Jesus wasn't born in Australia because there aren't any virgins. But what are you talking about? Why are they fighting? Archetypes? I'm afraid I don't understand. Which virgin and which whore? Asking who would win is like asking who's taller, the Australian or the American, isn't it? Can you show me what you've written? No? You're asking for my expertise and trying to draw me in, but not giving me much to go on. I don't know that I can help you. I'm sorry, this is a long-distance call for you, isn't it?"

—Australian "Fighting Father" Dave Smith, priest, author of Sex, the Ring, and the Eucharist, sixth-degree black belt, and pro boxer

FIGHT

The Whore is whupping some innocent ass when she is struck by a lightning bolt and killed instantly.

WINNER

VIRGIN (ACT OF GOD)

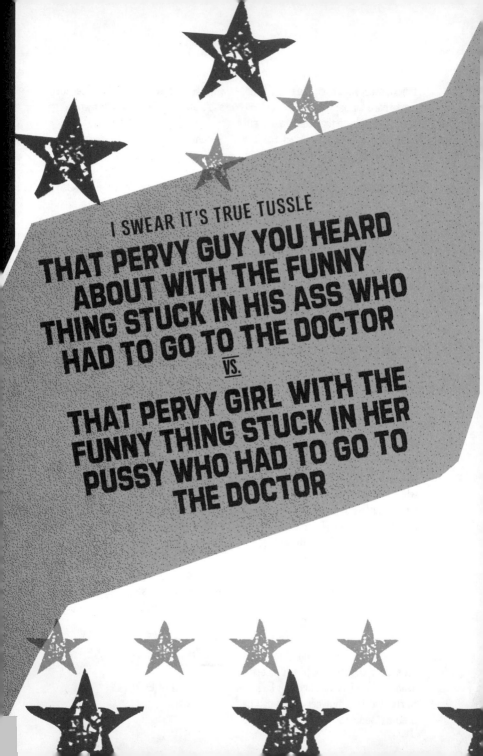

PERVY GUY WITH THING IN ASS

ALLY: Doctor who showed great dexterity in removing the foreign object and great discretion in not discussing it

ENEMIES: The nurses, who apparently all have blogs

PROBLEM: He's a classic overachiever, and this time he really shouldn't have tried to go that extra inch.

PERK: At least everybody knows about him now.

FROM NOW ON: He will only take his parsnips orally.

WHERE HE WENT WRONG: The Genoa salami up in there was cool; it's when he tried to add the Provolone cheese and roasted peppers that he ran into some trouble.

IF HE COULD DO IT OVER AGAIN: He'd probably go with an eraser over a sharpened pencil.

WHAT SHOULD HAVE OCCURRED TO HIM: At some point, the mouse will wake up and be really pissed.

PERVY GIRL WITH THING IN PUSSY

ALLIES: Boys who now know she's kinky as hell and are talking to her more than ever

ENEMIES: The boys who discover she'll stick *that* in her but won't grant them entry

PROBLEM: Who knew it was toxic?

PERK: If she ever is able to have a child after this, at least it will have something to play with in the womb.

FROM NOW ON: She will only use butter knives for cutting and spreading butter.

WHERE SHE WENT WRONG: Sometimes lightbulbs break.

IF SHE COULD DO IT OVER AGAIN: She'd lubricate the zucchini.

WHAT SHOULD HAVE OCCURRED TO HER: Sunday school's going to be awful awkward.

THE FIGHT

In a bout every junior high school student in America watches on pay-per-view, both combatants have great difficulty moving due to the foreign objects in their intimate areas. But the Pervy Girl has more room in her shame hole, which allows her greater mobility to dance around peppering the Pervy Guy with jabs until he is forced to retire due to profound anal fissures and humiliation.

THE WINNER

THAT PERVY GIRL (TKO)

LIFE CYCLE CRUSADE
STORK
<u>VS.</u>
GRIM REAPER

STORK

SYMBOLIZES: Parents' inability to talk about sex with their children

ALLIES: Uncomfortable adults

ENEMIES: Sex-education teachers

CHARACTERISTICS: Migratory; constantly in search of the best deals on babies

NESTS: Very large, to keep babies returned to sender

MATING: *Mostly* monogamous, just like Daddy

QUESTION #1: Isn't there a better way for the stork to deliver the baby than through Mommy's uterus?

QUESTION #2: Does that mean the stork fucked Mommy?

ADOPTION: The stork delivered the baby to the wrong address.

DOWN SYNDROME: The stork dropped the baby on its head.

MISCARRIAGE: The stork murdered the baby.

GRIM REAPER

HOBBIES: Reading Tarot cards; screwing with people who aren't really dying

ALLIES: Satan; Father Time; his fellow Horsemen of the Apocalypse

ENEMIES: Folks who aren't quite ready yet

TRADEMARK FIGHTING MOVE: The Fatal Finger

ENJOYS: Pestilence; plagues

LEAST FAVORITE PHRASE: "He's going to a better place." This is only necessarily true if he lives in Knoxville, Tennessee.

LOVE INTEREST: Sylvia Plath, although she can be a bit of a downer

COMPLAINT: Everybody wants to negotiate.

MISCONCEPTION: He won't play chess with you, no matter what Ingmar Bergman says.

FAVORITE SONGS: "Don't Fear the Reaper"; "MMM Bop"

THE FIGHT

The Grim Reaper, a huge favorite, is shocked when the Stork begins flinging babies at him. He whines to the judges to make the bird stop, but baby-flinging is ruled legal, and, as the Angel of Death, the Reaper is forced to kill each baby. But nonstop infanticide is too much for even him to take, and he skulks off shaking his head.

THE WINNER

STORK (DECISION)

SELF-HELP GURU

ALLIES: The insecure

ENEMIES: People who don't want you to be all you can be

TRADEMARK FIGHTING MOVE: The Punch of Positivity

OCCUPATIONS: Life coach; motivational speaker

FIGHTING ADVANTAGE: Knows opponent's needs, desires.

PAST: Used to be fat, dumb, lazy, depressed.

ADVICE: Visualize success and you'll achieve it. That'll be $89.99, payable in six easy installments.

TRIUMPH: Overcame amazing obstacles to achieve inspiring success.

MISSION: To help you help yourself.

DENIES: He has the same stupid problems you do.

FAILURE

ALLIES: Self-help gurus

ENEMIES: Kind of feel bad for him

TRADEMARK FIGHTING MOVE: The Unemployment Uppercut

OCCUPATION: He talked to this guy about this thing, but the guy never called back.

FIGHTING ADVANTAGES: A lifetime of frustration at his disposal, plus a lot of free time to practice with nunchucks

PRESENT: Currently fat, dumb, lazy, depressed

ADVICE: Don't do what I did, which was mostly nothing, but with a little fucking up sprinkled in.

TRIUMPH: Overcame the Gary Gnus for fourth place in the Great Space Coaster Fantasy Football League.

MISSION: To create a lifelike robot that can go to the unemployment office for him.

DENIES: He pissed in your chili, although your chili tastes like piss and he can't stop giggling.

THE FIGHT

The Failure brings his friends, a legion of fellow disappointments and embarrassments, to see the Self-Help Guru. They all take seats and pay thirty bucks to hear the Guru speak. Inspired by his message, the Failures visualize beating the Self-Help Guru to death with his own book, and then they go out and achieve their dream.

THE WINNER

FAILURE (KO)

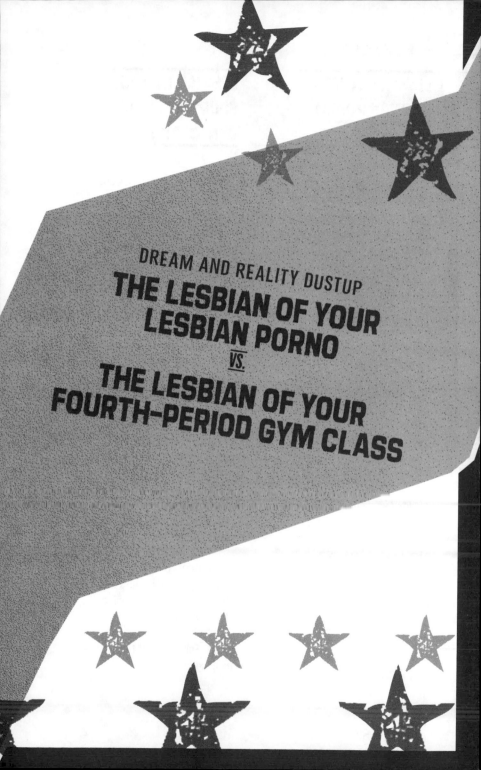

DREAM AND REALITY DUSTUP
THE LESBIAN OF YOUR LESBIAN PORNO
vs.
THE LESBIAN OF YOUR FOURTH-PERIOD GYM CLASS

LESBIAN OF YOUR LESBIAN PORNO

ALLIES: Millions of masturbators all over the world

ENEMIES: Engage her in cat-fights that take a decidedly carnal turn, making you the big winner.

FAVORITE ACTIVITY: Touching herself while looking at you

PROBLEM: Her boyfriend is out of town and she just doesn't know what to do. Her friend's coming over to console her. That should help.

OUTFIT: Shirt cut off to expose the underside of her breasts, a butterfly tattoo below her belly, and her red thong panties

DESIRE: Ménage à trois with you and her best friend

SECRET: She's been watching her roommate get it on with her boyfriend, and it makes her hotter and wetter than a tropical rainforest.

LESBIAN OF YOUR FOURTH-PERIOD GYM CLASS

ALLY: Fellow gym teacher aptly named Moose

ENEMIES: The unathletic; the pudgy; the slow; anyone who went through puberty too early or too late

FAVORITE ACTIVITY: Forcing you to play freeze tag, then teasing you mercilessly when you are it for thirty-seven minutes, until some acne-ridden freshman feels sorry for you and runs directly into your hand.

PROBLEM: Clearly never fully grasped the English language, as evidenced by her use of "youse" in sentences, such as "today youse is going to play kickball, whether youse like it or not."

OUTFIT: Gray college field hockey T-shirt, green and white short shorts, tube socks, running shoes, whistle

DESIRE: For youse all to do some jumping jacks

LESBIAN OF YOUR PORNO

SEXUAL INTERCOURSE: Involves much intimate exploration and is extremely naughty.

LESBIAN OF YOUR GYM CLASS

SECRET: She was dating your biology teacher, the one with the pendulous breasts, the little mustache, and the big varicose veins.

SEXUAL INTERCOURSE: Made disturbing use of the gym's Wiffle ball bat.

THE FIGHT

Though the Lesbian of Your Lesbian Porno tries to seduce the Lesbian of Your Fourth-Period Gym Class, the Lesbian of Your Fourth-Period Gym Class is attracted only to pear-shaped women with mullets. She beans the Lesbian of Your Lesbian Porno repeatedly with a dodgeball, then makes her do forty push-ups while she discusses her soccer team's midfield game with Moose. The Lesbian of Your Lesbian Porno just wants a little intimacy, merely a few soft caresses, but she is instead pegged in the head with a football and bashed in the face with a badminton racket until she is unconscious.

THE WINNER

LESBIAN OF YOUR FOURTH-PERIOD GYM CLASS (KO)

FIGHTS
FOR OUR WORLD

★ **BATTLES THAT DETERMINE THE ULTIMATE DIRECTION OF OUR SOCIETY**

EUROPEAN DRAGON

APPEARANCE: Huge, scaly, and fire-breathing, with wings, legs, and an extremely long tail due to enhancement surgery

DISPOSITION: Evil, especially when you forget anniversaries

DEPICTIONS: Often guarding cursed treasure, which is the shittiest kind of treasure

ITALIAN DRAGON: Hits on women constantly, gesticulates, has a strangely lucrative career in waste management.

BULGARIAN DRAGON: Wears funny polyester shirts, has a mustache, smells like yogurt and grease.

CELTIC DRAGON: Needs someone to drive it home from the bar

RUSSIAN DRAGON: Takes bribes.

POLISH DRAGON: Stopped using vibrators because it chipped its teeth. Owns a solar-powered flashlight. Froze to death waiting outside to see the movie *Closed for Winter.*

GERMAN DRAGON: Not comfortable discussing its past.

ASIAN DRAGON

APPEARANCE: Trunk of a snake, scales of a carp, tail of a whale, antlers of a stag, face of a camel, talons of an eagle, ears of a bull, feet of a tiger, eyes of a lobster, and the impeccable fashion sense of Miss Reese Witherspoon

DISPOSITION: Overbearing and bossy but kindhearted, like a Jewish mother

DEPICTIONS: There are nine classical types of dragons in Chinese mythology, each of which could kick your ass in trigonometry.

CHINESE DRAGON: Contains MSG.

VIETNAMESE DRAGON: Hides in bushes; is a Communist.

JAPANESE DRAGON: Enjoys buying used panties from vending machines and looking up skirts with the tiny camera on its shoe.

KOREAN DRAGON: Trying to get the bomb

POLITICAL SYMBOLISM: For the unwavering power of the Empire, my dong

EUROPEAN DRAGON

JEWISH DRAGON: Just ripped you off. Generally prefers litigation to battle, excepting one legendary Ashkenazi trouser dragon, which has vanquished many a lass, believe you me.

BLOOD: Has magical properties, like my semen.

RESIDENCES: Lives in underground lairs and all the lovely ladies' fantasies.

LEGEND: Says the Dragon holds the princess captive— although, if you ask me, she sure don't look like she wants to leave.

ASIAN DRAGON

AGRICULTURAL SYMBOLISM: Foreshadows the coming of rain. That's white rain, ladies. You heard me.

ORB: Occasionally the dragon is seen with an orb, and whosoever holds the orb becomes omnipotent. Whosoever cups, caresses, and gently licks the orbs becomes even more omnipotent. You know what the hell I'm talking about.

ALLIES: The Emperor; that yoga teacher who put her legs behind her head, which sounds weird but is totally hot

ENEMIES: Tigers; prudes

TABOO: It is a no-no to mess with the depiction of a dragon: A Nike ad showing LeBron James slaying a dragon was immediately censored by the Chinese government. Female infanticide—that they'll let go. But don't fuck with the dragon.

EXPERT ANALYSIS

"Asian Dragons bring good luck if you were born in the correct year. They also get jerked around mounted on poles in more than 500 parades each year. Too often, they distract and block a film's hero while his opium-smuggling quarry gets away, vanishing into the back alleys of Hong Kong or Chinatown.

"European Dragons get voiced by Sean Connery and battle Saint George. They strike terror in the hearts of Sinbad and Douglas Fairbanks with a half-glimpsed claw and a cheesy jet of flame. They participate in medieval warfare, setting fire to the catapults, the catapult ammunition, and the catapult operators.

"But was Bruce Lee ever likened to a European Dragon? No. Asian Dragon wins."

—Dale Dobson, humorist for
Cracked, National Lampoon, and
Yankee Pot Roast

"If a European Dragon and an Asian Dragon got into a fight, there's no doubt in my mind which would win. The European Dragon, with its long, scaly body and bat-like wings, would be a little bitch to catch—flapping and zipping around; breathing a constant stream of fire. But the smart Asian Dragon would dodge this scattered rage, let him tire himself out, and then, all of a sudden, command the forces of his celestial powers to change the weather . . . thus blowing the European Dragon all the way to outer space."

—Natalie Inger, content contributor for www.Draconian.com, the online source for everything you want to know about dragons

"It's not even a contest. Asian Dragons are exotic, elegant, and beautiful. European Dragons are boring and ugly."

—My friend Dan K., who dates only Asian girls but won't call it a fetish

THE FIGHT

The Asian Dragon trains fourteen hours a day for five years for this battle, but then the European Dragon refuses to fight, as it is on a six-week summer vacation on the French Riviera from its part-time job doing nothing.

THE WINNER

ASIAN DRAGON (DQ, LAZINESS)

BATTLE FOR THE DREAM HOUSE

BARBIE
vs.
KEN

BARBIE

ALLIES: Millions of little girls who hope that one day they, too, can be an astronaut with a nineteen-inch waist

ENEMIES: Feminists

SALES: Over a billion dollars a year

EVERY SECOND: Three Barbies are sold.

PERCENTAGE OF GIRLS WITH BARBIES: 95 percent; the other 5 percent are unloved

VISITORS TO THE BARBIE WEBSITE: 51 million per month

HEIGHT: $11\frac{1}{2}$ inches

WEIGHT: Light, like all girls should be

DISTINGUISHING FEATURES: Ginormous breasts, teensy waist

RESIDENCE: Dream House™

HOBBIES: Modeling; purging; laughing on the outside and crying on the inside

COLLECTORS: Often gay men

KEN

ALLY: That funny little boy who wears his mommy's lipstick

ENEMY: My Buddy™, who is surprisingly belligerent

SALES: 75 percent discount at a gay man's tag sale

EVERY SECOND: He makes a little boy a homosexual.

PERCENTAGE OF GIRLS WHOSE FIRST IMAGINARY BOYFRIEND IS GAY: 95 percent

VISITORS TO KEN'S ANONYMOUS "MEN SEEKING MEN" CRAIGSLIST POSTING: 147

HEIGHT: $11\frac{1}{2}$ inches

WEIGHT: Heavy with the burden of servitude

DISTINGUISHING FEATURE: Crotchless crotch

RESIDENCE: YMCA in the Castro

HOBBIES: Going to the tanning salon; trying on Barbie's clothing

COLLECTORS: Exclusively gay men

BARBIE

FULL NAME: Barbie Millicent Roberts™

ORIGIN: Created in 1959, based on a German fetish doll for adults named Bild Lilli and named after creator Ruth Handler's daughter Barbara. Really.

LOW POINT: In 1992, Talking Barbie fueled ugly gender stereotypes by proclaiming "math class is tough" and "will we ever have enough clothes?" — which, when you think about it, is an excellent question.

FUNDAMENTAL QUESTION: Why aren't you skinnier and prettier, little girl?

EXISTENCE: Controversial but profoundly influential, like the atom bomb

KEN

FULL NAME: Ken Carson™

ORIGIN: Created in 1961 due to wild demand for a boyfriend for Barbie, and named after Ruth Handler's son Kenneth. Really.

LOW POINT: 1993's Earring Magic Ken™ had a pierced ear, highlighted hair, lavender vest, and silver-ring necklace (swear to God), giving its young and impressionable female owners a complete misperception of what a straight man looks like.

FUNDAMENTAL QUESTIONS: Why am I not like the other boys? What do these strange feelings mean?

EXISTENCE: Necessary but bemoaned, like maxipads

EXPERT ANALYSIS

"It has been pointed out that if Barbie were a human-sized woman, she would be 7'2", weigh no more than 130 pounds, and have a 38–48 inch bust. This— plus the fact that her tiny feet are permanently molded into a high-heel position—gives her a hilariously poor center of balance, making her likely to topple over in a fight. Still, Barbie has managed careers as a ballerina, fashion model, firefighter, a WNBA player, and President of the United States.

Other than more body mass, Ken's only advantage seems to be that he has underwear permanently molded to his body, preventing wedgies. Also, in case backup is needed: Barbie has WAY more friends, many of them from Malibu. The winner? Undoubtedly Barbie."

—Jennifer Dzuria, stand-up comedienne, blogger (www.jenisfamous.com)

"In real life Ken would have kicked his sister's ass any day. I think in the realm of dolls he would have been satisfied with just donkey punching her."

—Jeff Handler, son of Kenneth (Ken) Handler, nephew of Barbara (Barbie) Handler. Really.

"I think that Barbie would win, because Ken is too prissy, and Barbie probably had some kind of kung-fu lessons or something like that."

—Lindsey Doublet, age ten

THE FIGHT

Hi, little girls! It's Barbie! I love you, let's go shopping. Did you know we girls can do anything™? It's true! Today I ate, I slept, and I shopped. Okay, I didn't eat! But you should, if you're not scared of getting fat! Boy, things are great in my Dream House™! Did you know I have a magic pony in my bedroom? You should ask your parents for a magic pony. If they don't buy you one, they don't love you! My friends bought me the pony because I'm so pretty. I hope you're pretty, because if you're not you'll die alone! Hey, you know what's gross? Little ugly girls! Oh, and going to the bathroom. Ewwww! Don't do it.

Today Ken came over to the Dream House™ with his friend Alan, and they were holding hands like little kids! But they're not little kids! Ken said, "Barbie, what are you doing home? I thought you were an astronaut this week." But this week I'm a princess! Then Ken pushed me out the window. Good thing I can fly! You can, too. We girls can do anything™! I flew by the Dream House™ window and I looked in and saw Ken laughing and tickling Alan's funny place. You know what else? They were not wearing pants. Gosh, it's not that warm in the Dream House™!

I flew back in the window and Ken said "Why don't you die?" I don't know! That was when Ken and Alan poured the gasoline on me and tried to set me on fire. Good thing I'm flame resistant! You are too. Alan started crying and ran out of the Dream House™. I wonder what was wrong. Ken also left, except he didn't use the door, he jumped out the window. Silly! I thought maybe he just wanted to fly around for a while. But you know what's weird? Ken can't fly.

THE WINNER

BARBIE (KO)

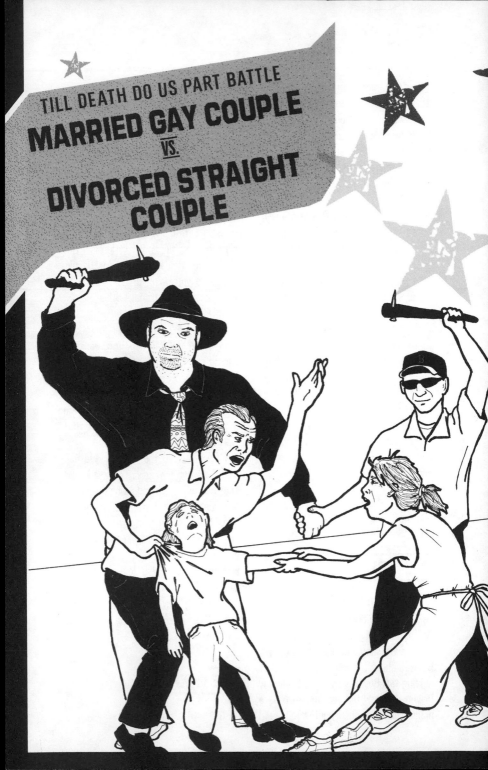

MARRIED GAY COUPLE*

STRENGTH: Sharing gender, deep love makes them battle as one.

WEAKNESS: They cannot look to God for help.

PROBLEM: The parts don't fit.

DANGER: They will get their gay on you.

ARGUMENT AGAINST SAME-SEX MARRIAGE: What's next, letting someone marry their pet? Their baby? What if a gay marries you against your will?

RELATIONSHIP TO TRADITIONAL VALUES: They destroy the great tradition of marriage.

THEIR CHILDREN: Are teased mercilessly, because they have two daddies

ALLIES: Godless liberals; unmarried homos; homo-sympathizers

ENEMIES: The Lord, His assault rifle, and His crumpled cans of Coors Light

DIVORCED STRAIGHT COUPLE

STRENGTH: Extensive battle experience, with each other

WEAKNESS: They cannot look to each other for help.

PROBLEM: The people don't fit.

DANGER: Children told to ask Daddy why he's a worthless sack of shit and Mommy why she's a whore.

ARGUMENT AGAINST DIVORCE: It's important to keep marriages together to build a truly deep, meaningful bond of mutual resentment.

RELATIONSHIP TO TRADITIONAL VALUES: They uphold the great tradition of divorce.

THEIR CHILDREN: Are teased mercilessly, because they're children.

ALLIES: Divorce lawyers; self-help authors (women); strip club owners (men)

*The illustration on the previous page shows the author as a gigantic married gay. Illustrator Chris Frost thought this would be a funny joke, though Jake Kalish is neither married nor homosexual, and is also way cuter than Frost would have you believe. Jake (The Heterosexual) Kalish would like the women of the world to know he may be the least gay man alive, and asks that his friends please stop teasing him.

MARRIED GAY COUPLE

WHERE GAY MARRIAGE IS LEGAL:
Massachusetts, Navajo for
"Fairyland"

ADVOCATES' DEFINITION OF MARRIAGE:
See it as a legal right that
should be open to same-sex
couples.

ENEMIES' DEFINITION OF MARRIAGE:
See it as a natural right that
should be restricted from
buggering pervs.

MARRIAGE ADVANTAGE: Expresses
the depth of your commitment
to your domestic partner.

ALTERNATIVES TO GAY MARRIAGE: Civil
unions; de-gayifying yourself
like Elton John did when he
married that woman in the '80s

DIVORCED STRAIGHT COUPLE

ENEMIES: Each other

WHERE DIVORCE IS ILLEGAL: The
Philippines and Malta, where
they truly believe in the
sanctity of marriage

DIVORCE RATES: Increased
markedly in the twentieth
century, when the stars of film
and television showed married
people just how fucking ugly
and dumb their spouses were.

WAY TO LOWER DIVORCE RATES: Stop
marrying assholes.

DIVORCE ADVANTAGE: Easier than
taking off the ring every time
you go out.

ALTERNATIVE TO DIVORCE:
Annulment, Giuliani-style

EXPERT ANALYSIS

Declined to comment: Elton John, Rosie
O'Donnell, Ike and Tina Turner

"In calling this matchup, first examine
each side's available resources—the
Married Gay Couple probably has more
money, because divorces are expensive,
and the gay couple is statistically less
likely to have frittered away their dual
income on kids, simply by virtue of the

improbability of having had children accidentally. The straight couple is perhaps more likely to contain a physically intimidating construction worker (of the non-Village People phylum), but the gay couple is perhaps more likely to contain a hairdresser with access to a variety of sharp objects. A toss-up. The gay couple, however, is still together, and thus able to work in tandem in a fight. The straight couple is just as likely to turn their enmity on each other as to turn it outward. While many are familiar with the 'crane pose' that brought the Karate Kid victory, fewer are familiar with the fighting move in which one side distracts the other into reopening its custody battle. Go gay!"

—Jennifer Dziura, comedienne, blogger (www.jenisfamous.com), and divorced heterosexual

"I believe the 'battle' will be won by the Hollywood media and the gay couples. I know without a doubt the war will be won by Christians—of which neither of the aforementioned are."

—Rachel Pendergraft, national spokeswoman, Ku Klux Klan, who was also asked to comment on Hollywood Liberals and The Jewish Media vs. Honest, Hardworking Americans

THE FIGHT

The Married Gays come into the fight in much better condition, having taken advantage of their Crunch membership and fully organic diet. The divorced man is drunk and has hepatitis C he caught from his secretary. The divorced woman is fat and crying. Already overmatched, the Divorced Couple does not help their cause by bickering and trying to get their eight-year-old son to fight for them. The Married Gays dispatch their foes handily, albeit in an effeminate, whimsical, and aesthetically pleasing manner. Then they help the Divorced Couple decorate their separate apartments, and adopt their son.

THE WINNER

MARRIED GAY COUPLE (KO)

DUNGEONS AND DRAGONS PLAYERS

CIVILIAN IDENTITIES: Physics Club members; computer technicians; Klingon speakers

POPULATION: 20 million players worldwide (game published in fourteen languages)

ATYPICALLY TOUGH REPRESENTATIVE: Vin Diesel

COST OF HOBBY: About $30 for basic board game

GAME'S CLAIM TO FAME: World's first role-playing game

GAME'S VIRTUAL REALITY: A magical realm with dungeons, dragons

UNREALISTIC ASPECTS OF GAME: Severely overestimates the number of dragons in the world.

DEFENSES: Shields; Oxy cream; "I know you are, but what am I?"

PROBLEMS: Uncreative Dungeon Masters' constant quests to the same dungeon, where "all that stuff happens with monsters."

HEALTH CONCERN: Keeping dice-throwing arm iced, well rested

WORLD OF WARCRAFT PLAYERS

CIVILIAN IDENTITIES: Unknown, as they no longer actually interact with other humans.

POPULATION: 7.5 million players worldwide

ATYPICALLY TOUGH REPRESENTATIVE: Curt Schilling

COST OF HOBBY: About 50 cents a day, or how much it would cost to feed a starving African child

GAME'S CLAIM TO FAME: World's #1 social-skills destroyer; cause of Internet addiction

GAME'S VIRTUAL REALITY: A magical realm with dungeons, dragons

DEFENSES: "I'm really focusing on my character right now"; "I didn't want to date her anyway"; "Oh yeah? Well, you wouldn't make it past Level Ten!"

PROBLEMS: Sylvanas Windrunner and Varimathras are engineering a new plague to wipe out all humans in Azeroth. Also, they have not seen a vagina since birth.

D&D PLAYERS

SOCIAL INTERACTION: Explore magical realms while eating Domino's together.

SOCIAL FUNCTION: Allows the otherwise friendless to band together and imagine a world with dragons, without acne.

SOCIAL TRAINING: Prepares young adults for future Dungeon Masters of the office.

SEXUAL RELATIONS: Virtual

AUTHORITY FIGURES: Dungeon Master; Mom

WEAPON OF CHOICE: Twenty-sided dice

SAD TRUTH: No one outside of D&D will ever refer to you as "Dungeon Master."

CRUEL IRONY: A 20 in charisma still won't get you girls.

WOW PLAYERS

SOCIAL INTERACTION: Virtual

SOCIAL FUNCTION: Allows dorks all over the world to unite without having to experience the discomfort of speaking to a person face-to-face.

SOCIAL TRAINING: Gets young men used to monthly fees in preparation for future Internet-porn addiction.

SEXUAL RELATIONS: Virtual

AUTHORITY FIGURES: Level-60 players; Mom

WEAPONS OF CHOICE: Mouse; keyboard

SAD TRUTHS: You can't take the fair maidens of Kalidor to the prom; not even Kel'Thuzad of Naxxramas will tell you where the clitoris is or what to do with it; and when someone asks where you've been all week, you can't say "The Plains of Mulgore."

CRUEL IRONY: He who can slay great beasts cannot undo bras, prevent wedgies.

EXPERT ANALYSIS

"The D&D players would be all 'I roll a 6 for my +2 magic spell . . .' but all us badass WoW players would be like 'CRITS MOTHERFUCKERS!' So there you have it."

—Barada, level-42 Orc Warrior, Draka server

"WoW! We have a bunch of crazy stoners on our side!"

—Redunment, level-60 Epic Shaman, Skywall server

"WoW all the way. I've played D&D, the only problem we'd have is with the monks from the book of exalted deeds. Fuckers."

—Dreamsower, level-60 Shaman, Skywall server

"D&D players because we have the benefit of exposure to real-life confrontation that is inevitable in a bad D&D game."

—Farmboymdp, member of the online Wizards Community of Dungeons & Dragons players

"We have a higher proportion of players who practice weapon arts. And the average player of D&D is more intelligent and creative than the average WoWser, due to the respective mental requirements of both games. And I myself am a competent practitioner of Tae Kwon Do."

—Toptomcat, Wizards Community

"In an actual war, WoW players would be equivalent to a large, powerful nation, with a large technological power base. D&D players would be equivalent to a well-run resistance cell. Individual engagements would vary, but we might be able to win by means of attrition."

—JasonOrlandoHawk, Wizards Community

THE FIGHT

Battling as the main event at the World Fantasy Convention, the WoW players enter the quest vastly outnumbering the D&D adherents, but, transfixed by their virtual universe, they are unable to look up from their laptops and are overwhelmed by a "surprise" direct attack and beaten senseless by Dungeon Master Guides and Monster Manuals.

THE WINNER

D&D PLAYERS (KO, SURPRISE DIRECT ATTACK)

CONSPIRACY THEORISTS

TOP SECRET #1: The CIA is responsible for 9/11, and then they couldn't figure out their own plan.

TOP SECRET #2: JFK shot himself.

TOP SECRET #3: Elvis is alive, and extremely lazy.

TOP SECRET #4: There's spermicide in malt liquor to control the African-American population, which explains why African-Americans never have babies.

EVIDENCE: Is fake, and for gullible suckers

TRUTH: Is hidden

JEWS: Kill Christian babies to make matzo, which is odd, as Christian babies are leavened.

FUNDAMENTAL PROBLEM: They assume people are capable of insidious secret plots, which most aren't. Except for Jews.

FUNDAMENTAL PROBLEM #2: Wouldn't a New World Order make things, you know, more orderly?

CONSPIRATORS

ALLIES: Move under cover of the night; hide in shadows.

ENEMIES: Conspiracy theorists, who know the truth behind the lies

TRADEMARK FIGHTING MOVE: Erasing your memory

VEHICLE: UFO

EVIDENCE: Destroys it

TRUTH: Is more horrible than you can imagine

JEWS: The six that run the world are dangerously braggy about it.

HOBBY #1: Watching your every move

HOBBY #2: Using bar codes to track you

HOBBY #3: Editing the new edition of *The Protocols of the Elders of Zion*

HANGOUTS: Underground bunkers; Masonic temples; The Skull & Bones Society

FUNDAMENTAL PROBLEM: Keeping everyone silent

CONSPIRACY THEORISTS

HOW TO MESS WITH ONE #1: Tell him you're off to an Illuminati meeting, and when he doesn't believe you, say "We knew you wouldn't."

HOW TO MESS WITH ONE #2: Tell him Nostradamus said something about him dying, but you forgot what.

HOW TO MESS WITH ONE #3: Tell him you can't meet Tuesday evening because Armageddon's scheduled for that morning.

HOW TO MESS WITH ONE #4: Tell him there are Masonic symbols hidden in the threads of Hillary Clinton's pantsuit.

GRAVITY: A government-imposed law to prevent us from freely floating into outer space.

ALLIES: Fellow kooks who believe lack of evidence *is* evidence.

ENEMY: The Man, who doesn't want you to know the real truth.

TRADEMARK FIGHTING MOVE: The Secret Society Slash

ANNOYING HABIT: Tendency to capitalize words like TRUTH, GOVERNMENT, and ALIENS on their Web pages.

CONSPIRATORS

THE SPACE PROGRAM: Faking the moon landing was tough; faking the *Challenger* explosion was damn near impossible.

VACATION SPOT: Area 51

POPULAR MISCONCEPTION: The spermicide isn't in the malt liquor, it's in the Kentucky Fried Chicken.

SAD TRUTH: The aliens would come, but they find you boring.

EXPERT ANALYSIS

"At first glance, this one seems simple—Conspiracy Theorists are angry, hungry, and want it more. But these guys spend a good amount of their time in their parents' basements, feverishly working the computer, jumping at shadows—when it all comes down to it, they're just Trekkies who've substituted flowcharts showing who controls the Federal Reserve for gay Kirk/Picard fan fiction. And you just know that the *actual* Conspirators—not just the average Jew, Freemason, or Ophthalmologist, but the ones who are *really* pulling the strings, are going to fight dirty as hell. Indeed, having given it a little thought, this one seems so easy to me, it makes me wonder why anyone would even question the outcome in the first place . . ."

—David Deutsch, humor editor for *Heeb* magazine and coauthor of *The Big Book of Jewish Conspiracies*

"If the fight was in the ring, it would depend on the boxers' respective corners. The Conspirator would take the advice of his trainer and cut man. The Conspiracy Theorist would ignore all advice and blame his defeat on aliens."

—Thom Burnett, author, *Conspiracy Encyclopedia* and *Who Really Runs the World?*

THE FIGHT

The Conspiracy Theorists are researching their opponents on the Internet, systematically uncovering all their secrets, when they suddenly die of unexplained circumstances.

THE WINNER

CONSPIRATORS (KO)

FIGHTER OF THE 20TH CENTURY BATTLE
MUHAMMAD ALI
VS.
BRUCE LEE

MUHAMMAD ALI

OCCUPATION: Boxer/poet

GIVEN NAME: Cassius Clay

ALLIES: The Honorable Elijah Muhammad; The Intolerable Howard Cosell

ENEMIES: George Foreman; Joe Frazier; Presidential Draft Board; Professional Boxing Commission

FIGHTING SIMILE: Float like a butterfly, sting like a bee.

FIGHTING STYLES: You can't hit what you can't see; rope-a-dope

COOL QUOTE #1: "Here I predict Mr. Liston's dismemberment. I'll hit him so hard he'll wonder where October and November went."

COOL QUOTE #2: "I have rassled with an alligator / I done tussled with a whale / I done locked up lightning / and thrown thunder in jail."

COOL QUOTE #3: "If Ali says a mosquito can pull a plow, don't ask how. Hitch him up!"

BRUCE LEE

OCCUPATION: Martial artist/ philosopher

GIVEN NAME: Li Jun Fan

ALLIES: Didn't need any.

ENEMIES: Often attacked one at a time, despite being in large groups.

FIGHTING SIMILE: Be like water.

FIGHTING STYLE: Emphasized the nontraditional "Style of No Style," which many men employ without knowing it.

COOL QUOTE #1: "True observation begins when one is devoid of set patterns."

COOL QUOTE #2: "If you put water into a cup, it becomes the cup. You put water into a bottle and it becomes the bottle. You put it in a teapot, it becomes the teapot. Now, water can flow or it can crash. Be water, my friend."

EMBARRASSING PERSONAL ANECDOTE THAT YOU WOULDN'T HAVE WANTED TO MENTION TO HIM DURING HIS PRIME: His mother named him Li Jun Fan, a girl's name, to ward off evil spirits that she believed attacked male children.

ALI

MOST CONTROVERSIAL QUOTE: "I ain't got no quarrel with the Vietcong . . . no Vietcong ever called me nigger."

EMBARRASSING PERSONAL ANECDOTE THAT YOU WOULDN'T HAVE WANTED TO MENTION TO HIM DURING HIS PRIME: The first time a girl kissed him, he fainted.

UNDERRATED FIGHTING SKILL: Able to withstand incredible punishment—fourteen rounds in stifling heat against Frazier, eight rounds of getting wailed on by Foreman, and being interviewed by Howard Cosell after every fight.

THE THRILLA IN MANILA: After Joe Frazier's trainer, Eddie Futch, refused to allow Frazier to fight the fifteenth round because his eyes were closing, Frazier never spoke to Futch again. Many think Ali couldn't have fought the fifteenth either, and after the fight he said, "This must be what death feels like."

EXPERIENCE FIGHTING AN ASIAN: In 1976, Ali took on Japanese pro wrestler Antonio Inoki for $6 million. Most of the fifteen rounds Inoki was on his back kicking Ali's leg, and the fight was called a draw.

LEE

REASON THE UNITED STATES LOST THE VIETNAM WAR: Lee was considered physically unfit for the U.S. military because he had an undescended testicle.

UNDERRATED FIGHTING SKILL: Almost impossibly strong for a 140-pound man, could do two-finger push-ups.

MYSTERIOUS DEATH: He bit it in his mistress's house of a brain edema that an autopsy said was caused by a bad reaction to the prescription painkiller Equagesic. He could take Chuck Norris, but a pill brought him down?

RUMOR ABOUT HIS MYSTERIOUS DEATH #1: The prescription pills mixed badly with marijuana, which Lee liked to eat rather than smoke, and traces of which were found in his stomach.

RUMOR ABOUT HIS MYSTERIOUS DEATH #2: He overdosed on Spanish fly, which just sounds like something a thirteen-year-old made up.

RUMOR ABOUT HIS MYSTERIOUS DEATH #3: His demise was a delayed reaction to a Shaolin Monk's death touch.

ALI

INFLUENCE: Made white people fear large black men even more.

WHEN IN ROME: Won light-heavyweight gold medal at 1960 Rome Olympics.

MUSLIM CONNECTION: Is one.

PERCENTAGE OF MEN WHO HAVE PRETENDED TO BE HIM IN FRONT OF THEIR MIRRORS: 61

LEE

INFLUENCE: Made white people fear little Asian men.

WHEN IN ROME: Fought Chuck Norris in the Coliseum.

MUSLIM CONNECTION: Fought Kareem Abdul-Jabbar (actually a student of his) in *Game of Death.*

PERCENTAGE OF MEN WHO HAVE PRETENDED TO BE HIM IN FRONT OF THEIR MIRRORS: 112

EXPERT ANALYSIS

"Ali has the reality of actual combat experience in his corner, and a very long reach with substantial knockout power. On the other hand, Lee had intimate knowledge of the *one inch punch.* Lee would have some advantage with his kicking ability. Ali had a way of maneuvering his opponent into a corner by cutting the ring in sections and closing off escape routes. The toughness and resiliency of Lee's disposition and physical durability would be put to the test under the duress of repeated blows from Ali. Lee's best strategy would likely be to work kicks to the legs to take away the champ's ability to move fluidly and comfortably. Then Lee would be able to move inside Ali's reach and punch. If Lee was not allowed to kick to the legs, endurance would be his best strategy. At 80 pounds less than Ali, Lee would have an advantage of simply hauling around less weight than Ali. Also if he could get him swinging a lot, Ali's guns would get quite heavy although Ali is smarter than to allow a reverse rope-a-dope to occur. If Ali connected solidly I doubt anyone could withstand that sort of punishment very long, even Bruce Lee. The fight would hinge on two main points: one being the length and number of the rounds to completion; and two, whether Lee would be allowed to kick. If the length and number of rounds were short I would give the nod to Ali. If kicks were allowed the match would be more even. Split decision to Ali—Why? The strength, toughness, and experience of actual combat cannot be underestimated."

—Russell McCartney, seventh-degree black belt; writer for *Black Belt* magazine; founder and chief instructor, IWR and Peak Performance Sword Systems (www.ishyamaryu.com)

"This matchup demonstrates the cosmological principle of yin-yang. Flowing naturally, yin will eventually become yang and yang will become yin. At the beginning, Ali is floating like a butterfly (pure yin). Lee blasts away (pure yang), but Ali's softness protects against Lee's hard attacks. By the fight's end, Ali is throwing iron (pure yang) while Lee (now yin) simply vaporizes, remaining unscathed. This fight is the epitome of the Zen in martial arts, that once you realize all of life's opponents are really your partners, there can be no defeat—only recreation, discovery, and liberation. I have to call this 'fight' a draw. Note that just as the beginning and end of this 'fight' are illusions, Lee's death and Ali's solidity are also illusions. Both men will naturally recreate themselves in the wheel's next spin."

—Joseph Cardillo, author, *Be Like Water: Practical Wisdom from the Martial Arts*

"The only way Bruce Lee could win this fight is by turning Muhammad Ali's nuts into a speed bag using his infamous one-inch punch, gouging out his eyes, and biting off his nose. In other words, if it's a clean fight, Muhammad Ali. If it's a fight where anything goes, Bruce Lee."

—Erich Krauss, author with Dave Camarillo of *Guerrilla Jiu-Jitsu*

"I'm a Bruce Lee fanatic, but there is no way he beats Muhammad Ali. What people forget about Lee is that the man was five-foot-seven and weighed 135 pounds. When he sparred with his good friend Kareem Abdul Jabbar, Kareem gave the far more skilled Lee trouble because of his reach. Ali is six-foot-three with an 80-inch reach and, at his best, weighed 200 pounds. The young Ali was perhaps the fastest heavyweight ever. The old Ali, after he was slowed by his expulsion due to his opposition to the Vietnam War, was found to have the toughest chin perhaps in the history of the sport. Ali was also famous—or infamous—for fighting up or down to the level of his opposition. Against a legend like Lee, he would be ready. I love Bruce Lee. But against the Greatest, he would be merely second best."

—Dave Zirin, author, *The Muhammad Ali Handbook* and *What's my Name, Fool?": Sports and Resistance in the United States*

THE FIGHT

Ali tries the rope-a-dope strategy, but Lee, who is no dope, counters with the even more unconventional "kick-my dick" strategy, whereby he absorbs repeated battering of the groin in the hopes Ali will tire himself out or become confused. Finally, the champ sees an opening and throws a monster right cross at Lee, who spectacularly leaps over his fist, only to die in midair of mysterious circumstances.

THE WINNER

ALI (KO, UNEXPLAINED DEATH)

HOLLYWOOD LIBERALS

ALLIES: The Jewish Media

ENEMIES: People with core conservative values, like holding on to all their money and deporting the Mexicans

TRADEMARK FIGHTING MOVE: AIDS pin to the eye

CHILD: Tiny adorable African baby who goes perfectly with the drapes

HOPE: That there will be universal health care, and it will cover face-lifts

BATTLE EXPERIENCE: Fruitless and deafening arguments with Bill O'Reilly

CHARACTERISTICS: Better looking, smarter, and richer than you, but thankfully, they love the little people.

IDOL: Bill Clinton, up until he has sex with their women

ADVICE: Live Strong; Vote or Die; Save the Planet; See My Movie

HONEST, HARDWORKING AMERICANS*

ALLIES: Bill O'Reilly; Rush Limbaugh

ENEMIES: Insidious liberals who want to turn America into a land of gay Mexicans who perform free abortions in Spanish while on legalized marijuana

STRENGTH: They've got Bill O'Reilly, who just accused you of fucking a black, crack-smoking donkey. What? Deny it, then.

WEAKNESS: You can catch the religious ones when they're in trances, speaking in tongues.

TRADEMARK FIGHTING MOVE: The Tax Cut of Your Throat

WEAPON: Concealed handgun that will protect their family in the inevitable shoot-out with Bin Laden and Al Qaeda

ANNOYANCE: Persnickety Florida blacks in 2000 who wanted their "votes" to "count"

NOT HONEST OR HARDWORKING: Blacks; Hispanics

*Editor's note: Jake Kalish is neither honest nor hardworking, and resents those of you who are.

THE JEWISH MEDIA

ALLIES: Hollywood liberals; the government of Israel, which supplements their salaries

ENEMIES: People who actively seek the truth and find it from straight-shooting, unbiased sources like Fox News

TRADEMARK FIGHTING MOVE: The Information Deathgrip

SECRET: Six of them gather in a little room and divide up the thoughts in your head.

DIRTY TRICK #1: Hiding their horns with those funny caps, wigs

DIRTY TRICK #2: The Jews are also all the doctors and lawyers, which explains why nothing bad ever happens to Jews.

DIRTY TRICK #3: Jews are comedians and humor writers, so they can insidiously disarm you with laughter before taking over the world.

DIRTY TRICK #4: Even if you handcuff them, they will write by sticking their pens into the gigantic nostrils of their gigantic noses.

HARDWORKING BUT DISHONEST: Jews; Asians

HONEST BUT NOT HARDWORKING: Their children

NOT AMERICAN: Immigrants; anyone who disagrees

HOPE: Keep things the way they were in the good old days, but with lots more money this time around.

NIGHTMARE: Child will join a commune and subsist on homosexual lentils.

EXPERT ANALYSIS

Declined to comment: George Clooney, Barbra Streisand, Carl Bernstein, Larry King, Larry the Cable Guy, Jeff Foxworthy, Bill Engvall

"Against honest, hardworking Americans, the effete elites get beaten like baby seals. It will be a pyrrhic victory for Joe Sixpack, however. After their beating, the Hollywood Chosen will lick their wounds, stage a huge benefit for the survivors, and make a series of big-budget movies that depict themselves as martyrs and heroes (quite probably with Dakota Fanning as the character inspired by Harvey Weinstein), as well as a whole host of tie-ins, which aforesaid hardworking Americans will shell out innumerable shekels to see and own."

—David Deutsch, humor editor, *Heeb* magazine (www.heebmagazine.com)

"I believe the 'battle' will be won by the Hollywood media and the gay couples. I know without a doubt the war will be won by Christians—of which neither of the aforementioned are."

—Rachel Pendergraft, national spokeswoman, Ku Klux Klan, who was also asked to comment on Married Gay Couple vs. Divorced Straight Couple

THE FIGHT

The Hollywood Liberals send their assistants to fight for them, and the Jewish Media stands to the side, claiming to be impartial. Distracted by their Blackberries, the liberals' assistants are systematically lynched and blown away with shotguns. The Jewish Media describes this as a "heartless massacre" and the Hollywood Liberals have a fundraiser for the victims' families, hosted by Bono and Al Gore. With the trillions raised, the Hollywood Liberals and Jewish Media buy the United States and exile the Honest, Hardworking Americans to Cuba.

THE WINNER

HONEST, HARDWORKING AMERICANS (KO, BUT THEY LOSE IN THE END)

THE ULTIMATE WARRIOR

FORMS OF CONFLICT RESOLUTION: Pile drivers; body slams

CHARACTERISTICS: Is batshit crazy, jabbers nonsense, snorts loudly to punctuate his points

APPEARANCE: Painted face; bulging muscles

GREATEST MOMENT: Defeating Hulk Hogan in front of 67,678 fans at the Toronto Skydome in *Wrestlemania VI*

REAL NAME: Jim Hellwig

POST–WRESTLING CAREER: Outspoken advocate for the conservative agenda

TRADEMARK FIGHTING MOVES: Warrior Splash; Warrior Press

COMPLETELY NONSENSICAL QUOTE: "I look above to the Gods, and when you fall below the skeletons of Warriors past, the power of the Warriors will become the Eighth Wonder of the World."

QUOTE THAT FEELS LIKE IT SHOULD MAKE SENSE BUT DOESN'T: "A path with no obstacles doesn't lead anywhere."

THE ULTIMATE PACIFIST

FORMS OF CONFLICT RESOLUTION: Marches; sit-ins; protests

APPEARANCE: Skinny (from the fasting)

GREATEST MOMENT: Gandhi winning India's independence

HEROES: MLK; Gandhi

PRINCIPLED PACIFISM: Believes force is morally wrong.

PRAGMATIC PACIFISM: Believes there must be a better way than war.

QUESTION: WWJD?

ALLIES: The oppressed; hippies

ENEMIES: Oppressors; conservatives

MASCOTS: The dove; Dennis Kucinich

TRADEMARK FIGHTING MOVE: Not fighting

CONFUSING COUNTERARGUMENT: We must fight wars to preserve peace.

THE ULTIMATE WARRIOR

QUOTE THAT DOES MAKE SENSE BUT DOESN'T APPLY TO HIM: "There is nothing more intimidating and embarrassing than another human being who can kick your ass with their mind."

CONTROVERSIAL OPINION: "Queering doesn't make the world work."

NOTABLE ACCOMPLISHMENTS: Two-time Intercontinental Champion; one-time WWF (now WWE) champion

BOSS: The ever-considerate, socially responsible Vince McMahon

ALLIES: Sting (the wrestler, not the tantric-sex-having singer); Ann Coulter

ENEMIES: The Undertaker; Macho Man Savage; Hulk Hogan; homosexuals

ALIAS: Just goes by Warrior since 1993, to keep things simple.

SHORTCOMING: Has had great difficulty engaging in calm, intelligent conversation, due to his overwhelming 'roid rage and tendency to shake, scream, and slobber.

THE ULTIMATE PACIFIST

BETTER COUNTERARGUMENT: In certain situations, such as the rise of Hitler's Germany, it's slightly important to bring your guns.

QUOTED SCRIPTURE: Jesus' Sermon on the Mount, in which he says "turn the other cheek," which is holy and all, but sucks as a battle strategy.

PROBLEM WITH PACIFISM #1: Even when peace marches are totally, 100 percent right, it's not the type of crowd you want to be seen with.

PROBLEM WITH PACIFISM #2: Talking it out gets you tired. Punching it out gets you pumped!

PROBLEM WITH PACIFISM #3: Taking a horrible beating and still holding firm to one's principles is cool when someone else is doing it.

THE ULTIMATE WARRIOR

LITTLE-KNOWN FACT: He wrote a comic book that features him attacking the North Pole and forcing Santa into bondage gear. Really.

DVD: Released by the WWE in 2005 and titled *The Self-Destruction of the Ultimate Warrior*, which led to the Warrior filing a defamation lawsuit.

EXPERT ANALYSIS

"In general, I believe that a person who understands how to use nonviolent resistance will always 'win' against someone who understands only violence, but in the sense that the outcome of the conflict will be that the values of society will be moderated in the direction of the values of nonviolence (toward justice and love) rather than in the direction of violence (toward injustice and hate). Nonviolence does not guarantee the physical survival of the practitioner. This was Gandhi's view, and he understood nonviolent resistance mainly from a religious perspective. Secular interpretations of nonviolence, such as the psychological interpretation taken by Richard B. Gregg in his book *The Power of Nonviolence*, and Gene Sharp's political and historical interpretation in his book *The Politics of Nonviolent Action*, imply a similar invincibility to nonviolent resistance."

—Brad Lyttle, president, United States Pacifist Party (www.pacifistparty.org)

"I'm not quite sure what you're asking me to provide. But I have to start by questioning the premise that the pacifist is smaller and weaker. Maybe less belligerent but not necessarily less gutsy or feisty. Active nonviolence, relying on social power not violence, has often proven stronger not weaker. How else did Gandhi throw the British empire out of India or people of Central Europe bring down the Soviet empire? Nonviolent activism theorist Gene Sharp describes it as social jiu jitsu. If in your imaginary fight the Pacifist practices this, not only might he win, your story might actually be a lot more humorous. Think about it, do some more research into the practice of nonviolence, and get back to me."

—Gerald W. Schlabach, theology professor at the University of St. Thomas, and author of *Just Policing, Not War: An Alternative Response to World Violence*

"Dig your claws into my organs! Stretch into my tendons! Bury your anchors into my bones! For the power of the Warrior will always prevail!"

—The Ultimate Warrior, from a WWF interview

THE FIGHT

One hundred thousand fans pack the Astrodome to see "War and Peace: The Ultimate Throwdown." The Ultimate Warrior sprints into the ring, all tassels, war paint, and anabolic injections. The Ultimate Pacifist arrives holding a single white rose and wearing a sari. He gets clotheslined. And suplexed. And pile-driven. (Pile-drove?) The Pacifist does not raise a finger as he is beaten mercilessly, asking only for the chance to speak to the crowd. "Look inside your hearts," he pleads. "Isn't there a better, simpler solution?" There is a brief pause as all consider his words. Then the Warrior takes out his concealed handgun and shoots him to death.

THE WINNER

THE ULTIMATE WARRIOR (KO)

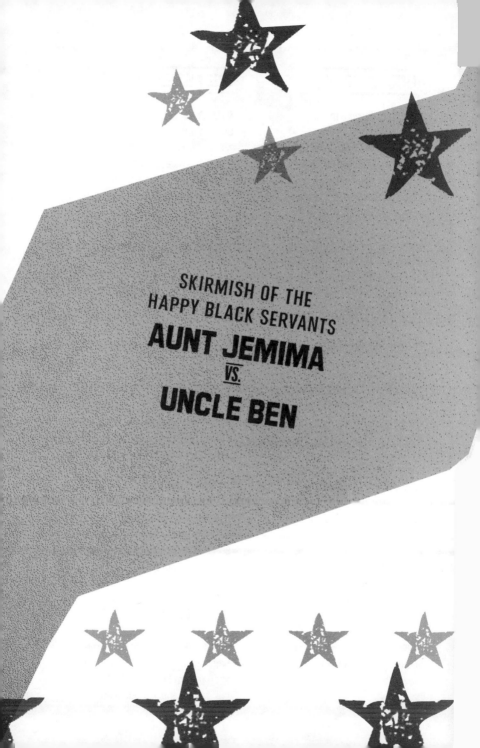

AUNT JEMIMA

STEREOTYPE: Servile mammy

PRODUCTS: Pancake flour; syrup; other breakfast products that don't need affirmative action to work their way up supermarket shelves

ORIGIN: The pancake mix debuted in 1889, or what the Klan calls "the good old years."

ALLIES: Fearful honkies

ENEMIES: Uppity Negroes

LOVES: Serving white people; the plantation on a hot summer day

HATES: Freedom

PHYSICAL CHARACTERISTICS: Plump, round face, charming smile, jungle booty

SCRAPPED SLOGAN: Syrup's better when it's oppressed!

TRADEMARK FIGHTING MOVE: The Breakfast Special, which involves your face and a frying pan.

FAVORITE SEX ACT: Interratio, or when she gives a white guy a blow job.

UNCLE BEN

STEREOTYPE: Servile old black man

PRODUCTS: Rice, related food products that don't need handouts or reparations

ORIGIN: Uncle Ben's started in 1943, because our boys overseas needed some racism.

ALLIES: Other nice blacks who aren't all boo-hoo whiny about 400 years of slavery, discrimination, and abuse

ENEMIES: NAACP

LOVES: Rice when it's cooked just right

HATES: A proper education

PHYSICAL CHARACTERISTICS: Twinkling eyes, charming smile, huge rice-stirring penis

SCRAPPED SLOGAN: You can whup me if the rice ain't fluffy!

TRADEMARK FIGHTING MOVE: The Grains of Pain

FAVORITE SEX ACT: Interratio from white woman, whom he must then pay to keep silent, lest her family and friends beat him to death.

AUNT JEMIMA

COMPETITION: Tia Miraflor, an Ecuadorian illegal who'll serve you pancakes in exchange for a sleeping bag in the walk-in closet, and not getting reported.

UPDATED IMAGE: No kerchief, thinner and cuter, wears pearls, isn't a slave

UNCLE BEN

COMPETITION: Farrakhan Rice— the rice that starts brown and only gets browner.

UPDATED IMAGE: Now he's "chairman" of the company, although, curiously, he is still called "Uncle" by white people.

THE FIGHT

White people win, again.

THE WINNER

NEITHER (DOUBLE DQ FOR INCORRECT SKIN COLOR)

COMPULSIVE GAMBLER

OCCUPATION: Doesn't matter — doesn't go anymore

SKILL: Able to completely disregard reason, mathematics, logic.

ALLIES: Employees of casinos, where he just keeps getting comped

ENEMIES: Unlucky dealers; evil cards; mean-spirited dice

LOVE INTEREST: That smoking-hot older chick who's totally into him but keeps asking for 200 bucks every time

BATTLE EXPERIENCE: Once tearfully convinced bookie not to break his "good" leg.

SUPERPOWER: Can make rent money disappear before his children's eyes.

ALIASES: Sucker; fish; embarrassment to his family

HOBBY: Taping episodes of *Jeopardy!*, watching them, then rewatching them and betting on the answers with unsuspecting suckers, who still somehow manage to win.

RACEHORSE

OCCUPATION: Athlete, albeit one allowed to shit in public

SKILL: Runs like the wind while tasting like beef.

ALLIES: Its jockey; gamblers with winning tickets

ENEMIES: Other jockeys; gamblers with losing tickets

LOVE INTERESTS: One gorgeous filly; two ugly stable hands with a video camera

BATTLE EXPERIENCE: Once took the Boy Wonder over the rails, but only because he was spreading rumors.

LOVED BY: Young girls and degenerates

ALIASES: Seabiscuit; Secretariat; Fucking Idiot Animal That Put My Family in Debt

PROBLEM: This little schmuck's always on its back.

TROUBLING QUESTION #1: My friend hurt his hoof. Why'd he get shot in the head?

TROUBLING QUESTION #2: I've got a huge penis, even for a horse. What am I hung like?

COMPULSIVE GAMBLER

PROMISE: He will pay you back as soon as this thing comes in.

LIE: It's all "worth it" to "pay" for "the excitement."

FAVORITE PHRASES: "Let it ride"; "I'm all in"; "Can I take that back?"

MEMORY: There was this one night in Reno he was a Golden God.

BLACKJACK TIP: Always split aces and eights unless you've got a real good feeling.

POKER TIPS: If a guy goes all-in, he's bluffing because he thinks he's smarter than you. Call him every time. Also, it's better to play poker on the Internet, because if you really have to piss you can go in a water bottle and never miss a hand.

CRAPS TIP: Funny thing, they won't let you gamble your plane ticket home.

BACCARAT TIP: It's fucking bullshit. Those Bond movies lie!

HORSERACING TIP: He got one on the filly in the sixth, and can't lose this time.

RACEHORSE

GOAL: To run until that little guy stops whipping me and shouting.

GREATEST ACCOMPLISHMENT: Secretariat winning the Belmont by thirty-one lengths, which would be man's greatest athletic accomplishment in history, had it not been done by a horse.

CHEATING FOR YOUR HORSE TO WIN: "Milkshaking," in which a mixture of water and baking soda is forced into the horse's system to slow the release of toxins into the bloodstream, preventing the horse from tiring.

CHEATING FOR THE OTHER HORSE TO LOSE: "Sponging," where small sponges are stuffed up horses' nostrils to restrict their breathing and slow them down.

DRUGS: Horses are illegally doped with uppers or steroids to win, downers to lose, Ritalin to write about it, and Prozac to deal with the stress.

COMPULSIVE GAMBLER

ROULETTE TIP: It's totally fixed, with, like, weights and magnets and magic spells.

SLOTS TIP: Fat Hispanic and black women always win. Sit next to one, then wait, wait, wait . . . mug her.

GENERAL TIP: If you get a dealer named Frank with a mustache, you will never lose.

EXCUSE: Was running good until this cocktail girl spilled his scotch and ruined his life.

EXPERT ANALYSIS

"This is absolutely no contest. The physically fit four-legged Racehorse literally stomps the brain dead Compulsive Gambler. I'm talking a skull crushing, bloody pulp, puree of human flesh, Wesley Willis 'wupped Superman's ass' stomping. This is the only time you will hear me say this, but bet the house payment and your life savings on Racehorse, who not only is a southpaw, but also a north, east and west paw. I don't even think Compulsive Gambler is dumb enough to bet on himself here."

—Chad Freeman, Las Vegas film critic and entertainment writer who runs the pop-culture Web site www.pollystaffle.com

"So I've got the nuts on the flop and this fish calls my all-in to draw to an inside straight, because he thinks I'm on a stone-cold bluff. Guess what hits on the river? Yeah, so I lost everything. What was the question?"

—Jay Kobkalish, compulsive gambler

"Can some desperate degenerate defeat me? Neigh!"

—Secretariat

THE FIGHT

Carefully assessing the odds, the Compulsive Gambler bets fifty bucks on himself at 10–1 against, while also putting a grand, at 100–1 odds, on the animal defeating him within a minute. He instantly takes a left hoof to the groin and a right hoof to the temple, receiving massive head and penile trauma. He screams, "I did it! I finally did it!" The judges confiscate his winning ticket, disqualify him for betting against himself, and he dies.

THE WINNER

RACEHORSE (TKO, PENILE TRAUMA)

DONALD DUCK

CHARACTERISTICS:
Anthropomorphic duck with a quick temper and a severe speech impediment

OUTFIT: Sailor shirt and no pants, like it's Fleet Week

DEBUT: 1934, in *The Wise Little Hen*

WORLD WAR II EXPLOITS: Was a war hero, as evidenced in *Sky Trooper* (1942) and *Commando Duck* (1944). Disney characters were constantly featured in films, posters, and advertisements promoting the American war effort.

ALLIES: Sometimes Mickey Mouse; Uncle Scrooge McDuck

ENEMIES: Neighbor Jones; Black Pete; Chip 'n' Dale

LOVE INTEREST: Daisy Duck, originally named Donna Duck

MIDDLE NAME: Fauntleroy

RESIDENCE: Supposedly Duckburg with nephews Huey, Dewey, and Louie, but actually spends most of his time in the Disney prefabricated town of Celebration, Florida.

DAFFY DUCK

CHARACTERISTICS:
Anthropomorphic Duck with know-it-all smirk, beak that rotates around head impossibly when shot

OUTFIT: Usually nude, sometimes dressed stupidly for others' enjoyment

DEBUT: 1937, in *Porky's Duck Hunt*

WORLD WAR II EXPLOITS: Shameful, as he attempted to dodge World War II conscription in *Draftee Daffy* (1945).

ALLY: Porky Pig, as a lawman in the Wild West in *Drip Along Daffy* (1951) and *My Little Duckaroo* (1954), as "Watkins" to his "Dorlock Homes" in *Deduce, You Say* (1956), and most notably as Friar Tuck to his Robin Hood in *Robin Hood Daffy* (1958)

ENEMIES: Bugs Bunny; Elmer Fudd; Marvin the Martian; the Tasmanian Devil

LOVE INTEREST: Bugs (when he dresses like a girl duck)

RESIDENCES: Sherwood Forest; Mars

DONALD DUCK

PERSONALITY: Explosive hothead who, much like Tony Soprano, has great difficulty articulating his true feelings.

TRADEMARK CATCHPHRASES: "Aw phooey!"; "Oh boy, oh boy, oh boy!"

TRADEMARK FIGHTING MOVE: The Disney Lawyer Copyright Infringement Lawsuit

OSCAR: Best Cartoon in 1943, for *Der Fuehrer's Face*, a propaganda film in which he has a nightmare he is a *Mein Kampf*-reading starving artillery factory worker in "Nutzi Land" forced to salute every time he sees a picture of Adolf Hitler. He wakes up in the shadow of the Statue of Liberty, glad to be in the U.S. of A.

FUN FACT: Used as mascot for the U. of Oregon Ducks.

BEST-KNOWN ILLUSTRATORS: Al Taliaferro; Carl Barks

VOICE: Clarence "Ducky" Nash, from 1934 to 1985

VALUE AS TEACHING TOOL: Appears in numerous educational films, like *Donald in Mathmagic Land* (1959).

DAFFY DUCK

PERSONALITY: Petty, jealous glory-seeker who refuses to accept second billing. Bill-ing? Get it? Hoo hoo!

TRADEMARK CATCHPHRASE: "You're deth-picable!"

TRADEMARK FIGHTING MOVE: Shooting self in face with supposedly unloaded gun

IN THE FUTURE: He is Duck Dodgers in the 24½ century.

LEGENDARY PERFORMANCE: In *Duck Amuck* (1951), the surreal Looney Toon where Daffy is tortured by an unseen animator, which might be the single greatest cartoon in history

BEST-KNOWN DIRECTOR: Chuck Jones

VOICE: Mel Blanc, from 1937 to 1989

VALUE AS TEACHING TOOL: Teaches children that sadism is funny.

EXPERT ANALYSIS

"It's obvious that Daffy would win over Donald, who's prone to losing his temper and therefore his judgment. Daffy has many of Donald's bad traits, and is also self-destructive in other ways. But he's a clever, cunning little twerp, and can easily take Donald in a fair fight—not that either of them would be particularly interested in fighting fair."

—Don Markstein,
www.toonopedia.com,
the Internet's "Vast Repository
of Toonological Knowledge"

"Daffy needs to put more trust in a consciousness beyond his own. Life, like martial arts, is about self-discovery. The bout with Donald provides him with the experiential evidence he requires to overcome previous insecurities. By trusting in the 'big picture,' it is easy to simply go with the flow, knowing that wherever you end up is exactly where you need to be. Your job is to look for the lesson within the experience, which Daffy now can do. He is not only the winner of this fight, but a winner in the ring of life. Finally realizing there are subtler forces influencing us than meet the eye, he will now have a much larger support system to help him generate success on all levels of living."

—Joseph Cardillo, author, *Be Like Water: Practical Wisdom from the Martial Arts*

"The Donald wins. No contest. The whole thing about Daffy Duck is that he's Sisyphus—none of his plans work and everything that can go wrong does. He's the Washington Generals of Looney Tunes. Furthermore, if Daffy plays dirty, like he often does, Uncle Scrooge can have him killed, just as he did with Speedy Gonzales."

—Ari Voukydis, commentator on *VH1: All Access* and one-half of the comedy team found at www.markandari.com

"Back in the late 1930s, before he went soft, Daffy Duck was a straight-up lunatic gangster. If the fight were to occur during that time period, the first minutes of battle would be a terrifying display of bloody feathers, of which the vast majority would belong to Donald. However, if Donald managed to survive the first assault and his Disney rage kicked in, he'd certainly get his licks. But in the end, I give it to Daffy by a landslide."

—Erich Krauss, author with Eddie Bravo of *Mastering the Rubber Guard*

"While a mutual lack of pants and no visible genitals might seem to level the playing field, there is no question that Daffy is the superior duck. What does Donald do in the face of adversity? Sputter and stammer and wave his stupid wings around. Big whoop. Daffy, on the other hand, tries to get a goddamn hunter to blast Bugs's bunny-hole off with a twelve gauge. That's some badass shit. Daffy might not always come out on top, but the message is clear: You do not fuck with that duck."

—Dan Bova, executive editor, *Maxim*

THE FIGHT

Donald smacks Daffy's beak around his face, then blows it clean off with a rifle. Daffy attempts to attack Donald with a quarterstaff, but instead hits himself in the face with it. Daffy tries to shoot an arrow at Donald, but accidentally fires himself from the bow directly into a tree. Donald is laughing hysterically and hollering unintelligible taunts at a frustrated and deflated Daffy when the large white-gloved hand of a rabbit erases him from existence.

THE WINNER

DAFFY DUCK (KO, CARTOONIST INTER-FERENCE)

FECES FRACAS

THE CONSTIPATED
vs.
THE INCONTINENT

THE CONSTIPATED

ALLIES: Bran muffin; wheat germ; Ex-Lax

ENEMY: The all-meat-loaf diet

SEVERE CONSTIPATION: Obstipation—as in "I'm all obstipated and can't squeeze out a joke here."

CAUSES OF CONSTIPATION: May be dietary, hormonal, could be a side effect of meds. He could have a greedy colon, which absorbs water too quickly, or a spastic colon, which spasms constantly. "Spastic Colon," incidentally—already taken as a band name.

EFFECT OF CONSTIPATION: A whole lot of sitting around doing nothing, wondering how he screwed up a basic bodily function that even the dumbest animals have mastered

CONSTIPATION IS COMPLICATED BY: Hemorrhoids; anal fissures. Yay! Anal fissures! Gimme an A! Gimme an N! . . .

STOOL: Hard, difficult to pass. Mostly, I just wanted one "stool" reference in my book.

THE INCONTINENT

ALLIES: Adult diaper and "protective underwear" manufacturers

ENEMY: The host of a dinner party ruined by a leaky rectum

GEOGRAPHY: The Incontinent must always be a short sprint away from a toilet.

CAUSES OF INCONTINENCE: Holding it in too long; severe abdominal strain; damage to the anal sphincter. Yeah! Anal sphincter! Goooooo, sphincter!

EFFECT OF INCONTINENCE: Romantic dinners suddenly get a hell of a lot less romantic.

GENDER SPLIT: Incontinence is more common in women than men, which explains all the freshening up.

NICKNAME: Doctor Dumpalot

DEFECOGRAPHY: A medical test that shows how much stool the rectum can hold, how effectively the rectum can hold that stool, and how well it can evacuate the stool. You win no prize if your rectum holds the most stool. Sorry.

THE CONSTIPATED

GENDER SPLIT: Women are more likely than men to be constipated, although men are ten times more likely to talk about it.

NICKNAME: Chock Full o' Feces

PARADOXICAL DIARRHEA: A sometime feature of obstipation, wherein soft stool from the small intestine bypasses the impacted feces in the colon. "Paradoxical Diarrhea" is still open as a band name. Go for it.

THE INCONTINENT

INCONTINENCE OFTEN OCCURS: During childbirth, so don't think something's gone horribly wrong with your baby.

THE FIGHT

Though both fecal fighters enter combat in a somewhat debilitated state, the Incontinent makes the counterintuitive but brilliant decision to charge pants-down and rectum-first, spraying ass-fire at his opponent. The Constipated is understandably disturbed by being slathered in feces, and is forced to concede defeat and retreat to the restroom to wipe himself off and face all of his failure.

THE WINNER

THE INCONTINENT (TKO)

UNDER THE INFLUENCE BATTLE
DRUNK
VS.
STONER

DRUNK

ALLIES: Bartenders

ENEMIES: Ex-girlfriends who receive 3 A.M. phone calls

COMMERCIALS: Only show those joyous moments of camaraderie that precede coming on to your friend's sister and pissing yourself.

TIME: Happy Hour, and other much less happy hours

JUSTIFICATION: If it's bad for you, why does it make you feel so good? You know, at least until the next day, when you feel like killing yourself and your family.

LETHAL COMBO: Liquor and pills

MEDICAL TREATMENT: Alcoholism is a disease cured by not drinking so goddamned much.

SEXUAL EFFECTS OF DRINKING: You find yourself explaining to the girl you never would have slept with sober why your penis doesn't work.

TRADEMARK FIGHTING MOVE: The Broken Budweiser Bottle Throat Stab

BATTLE CRY: "More gin in my gin!"

STONER

ALLIES: Weed dealers

ENEMIES: The hypocritical Establishment, dude

COMMERCIALS: Show that if you smoke marijuana, the terrorists will win and you will die.

TIME: 4:20

JUSTIFICATION: Nothing that naturally grows in the ground could ever be bad for you. You know, like poison ivy or hemlock.

LETHAL COMBO: Weed and work

MEDICAL TREATMENT: Medical marijuana cures cancer, makes people with glaucoma see things that aren't even there.

SEXUAL EFFECTS OF MARIJUANA USE: Sex just doesn't seem as fun as giggling about nothing and playing with your navel.

TRADEMARK FIGHTING MOVE: One-hitter upside your head

BATTLE CRY: "My tongue feels thick."

STAR ATHLETE: Ricky Williams

DRUNK	STONER
STAR ATHLETES: Mickey Mantle; John Daly	**PROPER SMOKING FORMATION:** Circle or semicircle, looking at one another
PROPER DRINKING FORMATION: Lined up at bar, staring into drinks	**FAUX PAS:** Drooling on the spliff
FAUX PAS: Vomiting on a stranger	**FILMS:** *Up in Smoke; Half Baked; Harold and Kumar Go to White Castle*
FILMS: *Lost Weekend; Leaving Las Vegas*	**SONGS:** "Legalize It"; "Puff the Magic Dragon"
SONGS: "Whiskey River"; "There Stands a Glass"	**HIGH WOMEN:** Sometimes make it out of the house.
DRUNK WOMEN: Sometimes make out with each other.	

EXPERT ANALYSIS

"Before considering the question of who would win an imaginary battle between a Drunk and a Stoner, we must first establish the identities of the parties under the influence. For instance, a celebrated stoner like the Black Crowes hippie-ish frontman Chris Robinson—who weighs about a buck o' five soaked with bong water—would likely wind up on his back faster than a one-legged hooker against the likes of a surly boozer such as the notorious star of *Gladiator*, who—while also a Crowe—is known more for ass-kickin' than kick-ass music. But who's to say that if Robinson were the one all jacked-up on vodka–Red Bulls and Crowe were higher than the price of real estate in Malibu, that the willowy Southern rocker might not land a lucky haymaker that would have Russell thinking HE'S the one who talks to angels? Then again, Robinson let Owen Wilson steal his wife . . . Owen Fuckin' Wilson?!!! Guy's funny as hell, but ain't the most masculine fella in the world. So I take it back—Russell Crowe beats the Black Crowe whether he's baked or boozy. In a related note, does anybody out there know where I can score some kine bud?"

—Dan Dunn, author of *Nobody Likes a Quitter (and other reasons to avoid rehab): The Loaded Life of an Outlaw Booze Writer*

"This seems like a no-brainer, but it could be a close call. Drunks shoot their wads. They spin and puff and chest-beat, but put Tom Waits on the jukebox and they'll be slinging their arm around your shoulder and lighting another Camel Menthol. If Stoners played it strategically, they could win. But let's face it. Stoners are peaceful. They don't want to fight. And the Drunks are gonna kick the ever-living shit out of them."

—Sarah Hepola, editor, www.salon.com

THE FIGHT

Both Drunk and Stoner are trampled by all the people trying to intervene on their behalf.

THE WINNER

NONE (DEATH BY INTERVENTION)

BATTLE OF THE SEXES
PAC-MAN
vs.
MS. PAC-MAN

PAC-MAN

INPUT: Joystick, which introduced young boys to the double entendre. ("Input" we got later, after porno viewing.)

VALUE: Created the video-game boom.

ORIGINAL NAME: Puck-Man, changed so vandals wouldn't change the *P* to an *F* (really)

SONG: "Pac-Man Fever"

UNSUBSTANTIATED RUMOR: Clandestine sexual relations with Q-Bert

HOBBY: Playing Pong

ALLIES: Most of the Space Invaders; Donkey Kong

ENEMIES: Funny colored ghosts; children's and young-adult authors

DEBUTS: Japan, 1979; United States, 1980

CREATOR: Toru Iwatani

DEVOURS: Power pellets, just like Barry Bonds

APPEARANCE: Yellow circle with a mouth

MS. PAC-MAN

INPUT: Hah! Input!

VALUE: Kind of made the Commodore 64 seem like a real computer.

ORIGIN: Created from one of Pac-Man's rib.

COMPARISON TO PAC-MAN: Faster and better, but still paid 70 percent as much, with less opportunity for promotion.

UNSUBSTANTIATED RUMOR: Both Mario Brothers at once

HOBBIES: Dancing; yoga; Pilates

IN SPARE TIME: Applies lipstick; puts on bow; writes secret love letters to Blinky

ALLIES: Frogger; Glass Joe from Punch-Out, who is so sweet despite his difficulties

ENEMIES: Inky; Pinky; Sue

DEVOURS: Power pellets; fruit; gender-based stereotypes

STRATEGY: Flirt with ghosts, watch them insult each other.

APPEARANCE: Yellow circle with lipstick, eyes, a mole

PAC-MAN

STRATEGY: Eat all four ghosts with one pellet.

HIGH SCORE: In 1999, Billy Mitchell of Hollywood, Florida, achieved a perfect score of 3,333,360 points, which, it turns out, is a feat not at all impressive to women.

SAD TRUTH: No matter how you run from your ghosts, they always eat you in the end.

TRAGIC FLAW: The final, or 256th, level is corrupted and unplayable, a discovery one can make only by wasting one's entire life.

SEQUELS: Ms. Pac-Man; Pac-Man Plus; Baby Pac-Man; Perverted Uncle Pac-Man; Developmentally Disabled Pac-Man; Tranny Surprise Pac-Man

MERCH: An endless array of T-shirts and toys; the ever-so-tasty Pac-Man pasta

MS. PAC-MAN

CHILDREN WITH PAC-MAN: Have her eyes, mostly because he doesn't have eyes.

TIRED LINE: "I got some power pellets for you."

SAD TRUTH: High score or no, you'll never understand her.

HIGH SCORE: 933,580 by Abdner Ashman of Pompano Beach, Florida, in 2006

TRAGIC FLAW: Arcade hardware crashes at or around 134th board, just right when you're both almost there.

CLAIM TO FAME: Your single most embarrassing masturbation fantasy

EXPERT ANALYSIS

"Like all working women, Ms. Pac-Man had to work far harder than her male counterpart to earn the same rewards: She had four more mazes to navigate and faster ghosts to elude, not to mention food that, like equal pay and a harassment-free workplace, actively eluded her. A hero for all modern women in a patriarchal society, Ms. Pac-Man fights for a cause, while her husband stumbles around mazes, popping pills and eating ghosts.

"Also, very few people know this, but Pac-Man has diabetes, so he's not as fast as he used to be."

—Ari Voukydis, *VH1: All Access* commentator and one-half of the comedy team found at the Web site www.markandari.com

"As arcade games, the original Pac-Man featured only one maze, repeated over and over again at increasing speeds until the screen split in half at the 256th level, whereas Ms. Pac-Man offered the variety of four different mazes of increasing difficulty. As actual competitors, Ms. Pac-Man's the only one who has eyes. Chomp chomp."

—Dave Itzkoff, science-fiction book reviewer, *New York Times;* editor, *New York Times* Sunday Styles section; author, *Lads: A Memoir of Manhood*

"Since most fights don't take place in cyberspace, both contestants would spiral to their sides like silver dollars the moment the bout began. However, if they could somehow find a way to inch toward one another, Pac-Man would be able to choke his female counterpart into unconsciousness using the pretty ribbon embedded in her scalp. If not for the ribbon . . . stalemate."

—Erich Krauss, author with Randy Couture of *Wrestling for Fighting*

"Pac-Man would not only defeat Ms. Pac-Man, but he'd go old-school nutty on her, domestic abuse style. And can you blame him? He's out busting his balls every day, eating blinking dots for a living with some prick kid running him into a wall all day long. What other job lists being chased by motherfucking spirits of the dead as a hazard? Then once you eat all the dots, guess what? More dots, asshole! The stress alone would make Pac-Man snap. The last thing he'd need is to come home and deal with his ugly wife. I mean, think about it: This is a race of people where the women are distinguished from the men by wearing a red bow on their heads. How would you feel if one small red bow was all that stood between you and womanhood? That much pent-up aggression would've even made Mother Teresa snap her leg off in someone's ass."

—Maddox, genius behind the *New York Times* bestseller *The Alphabet of Manliness* and visionary author of the best Web page in the universe: www.thebestpageintheuniverse.com

THE FIGHT

Moving at twice the speed of her male counterpart, deftly chomping on *moving* fruit and avoiding attacks from both male *and* female ghosts, Ms. Pac-Man is closing in on her overconfident misogynistic predecessor when he suddenly gets undeservedly promoted thirty-two screens by video-game manufacturers after a wild guy's night out at a strip club. With his new money and power, the eyeless wonder buys out Inky, Blinky, Pinky, and Clyde, who, after dogged pursuit, catch Ms. Pac-Man and eat her, preserving the status quo.

THE WINNER

PAC-MAN (KO, MEN RUN THINGS)

DISORDER DISPUTE
MANIC-DEPRESSIVE
VS.
OBSESSIVE-COMPULSIVE

MANIC-DEPRESSIVE

DEPRESSION: Characterized by persistent feelings of sadness, anxiety, guilt, isolation, and hopelessness, none of which will make you any fun at a keg party.

HYPOMANIA: An artistic state of the disorder, characterized by a torrent of creative thought and energy, like when I wrote a 500-page novel in a week from the perspective of a urinal cake.

STRENGTH: When manic they're unstoppable.

WEAKNESS: When depressed they're unstartable.

OBSESSIVE-COMPULSIVE

STRENGTHS: Will obsessively, compulsively study opponent's strengths, weaknesses prior to a fight.

WEAKNESSES: Will continue to obsessively, compulsively study opponent's strengths, weaknesses while actually fighting.

THE FIGHT

A Manic-Depressive man is ferociously pounding the crap out of an Obsessive-Compulsive when he suddenly becomes despondent and hides in a corner. The Obsessive-Compulsive takes advantage of this turn of events by tapping the Manic-Depressive's forehead thirty-nine times, but stops when he realizes he must immediately take a corresponding number of showers.

THE WINNER

DRAW (BOTH MEN IN NO CONDITION TO FIGHT)

MANIC-DEPRESSIVE

PROBLEM: The problem with psychiatric disorders is that a nervous and self-involved person feels he may have every one.

CHARACTERISTICS: Extreme mood swings (yup); difficulty in organizing or planning (uh-huh); lack of awareness (always); analytical nature (absolutely); inability to judge others' emotions (sure sounds like me); paranoia (they're talking about me again)

FAMOUS MANIC-DEPRESSIVE ARTIST: Vinny Van Gogh, although the posthumous diagnoses always seem a little fishy.

PARTS OF BRAIN AFFECTED: The I'll Rule the World Lobe; the I'm Never Getting Out of Bed Cortex

PREVALENCE: 6.4 percent, with enough symptoms for head doctors to cash in.

MANIA: Characterized by elation, euphoria, delusions of grandeur, and wildly impractical ideas, like when I tried to teach my dachshund Esperanto.

OBSESSIVE-COMPULSIVE

PROBLEM: Don't ask me, I'm counting paper clips.

CHARACTERISTICS: Distressing, intrusive thoughts (mustn't think about Mom giving blow job), followed by related compulsions or rituals to neutralize the obsessions (touch ceiling twelve times, pick four hairs from each nostril to stop thinking about Mom giving blow job)

FAMOUS OBSESSIVE-COMPULSIVE ARTIST: Michelangelo, which helps explain how the Sistine Chapel got done, but not how you'd diagnose someone with a psychiatric disorder 400 years before psychiatry.

PARTS OF BRAIN AFFECTED: Orbital-frontal cortex, which is contaminated and must be washed repeatedly.

PREVALENCE: Between 1 and 3 percent. Incidentally, both one and three are prime numbers, which means I must now do nineteen nude jumping jacks, then touch my perineum twenty-three times with each hand.

CELEBRITY PUBLICISTS

TOOL: Press release; promotional gift package

ROLE: Simultaneously cowtowing to the dicks in the media and the dicks who employ them.

PERKS: Get to annoy lots of semifamous people

SKILL: "Spin," which is itself spin on "lying"

OLD ADAGE: The only bad publicity is no publicity, which Pee-wee Herman might disagree with.

PROBLEM: Having to explain celebrity's coke- and booze-filled binges

ALLIES: Gossip columnists; celebrity magazines

ENEMIES: Gossip columnists and celebrity magazines when talking about the celebrity's anorexia sells more copies than talking about her baby.

TASK: Making one mediocre review of your client sound like four good ones.

PAPARAZZI

GOAL: Get an incredibly candid photo without getting punched.

INSTANT GOLD: First shots of a celebrity's new baby or new breasts

ALLIES: American Public, secretly

ENEMIES: American Public, publicly

STRANGE DEVELOPMENT: The same celebrity who spit at them when he had the #1 movie in America is begging them to take his picture now that he can't land a reality show.

CONFOUNDED BY: Female celebrity who wears no panties and spreads her legs to exit cars.

REGRET: They really shouldn't have called Gwyneth Paltrow's daughter Apple a "stupid little cunt" for covering her face and crying when they charged at her outside her preschool.

PROBLEM: One can get awful hungry hiding outside Lindsay Lohan's house for six hours.

TASK: Politely informing Courtney Love that her "half naked and out of it" photos have decreased in value, so she should probably put her top back on, wipe her nose, and go home to her teenage daughter.

CELEBRITY ASSISTANTS

TOOL: BlackBerry

ROLE: Do everything the celebrity doesn't want to be seen doing, like purchasing Imodium A-D.

PERKS: Get to live way beyond means

GOALS: Start own entertainment career or write a book about what assholes their famous bosses were.

SKILLS: Able to do laundry, organize schedule, and fax contracts all while being screamed at for purchasing the wrong body wash.

PROBLEM: Having to carry the celebrity in their arms from coke- and booze-filled binges.

ALLIES: C- and D-level celebrities looking to move up the ladder by bribing and/or having sex with them.

ENEMY: Their boss when the iced soy latte has too many or too few ice cubes.

TASKS: Screening fan mail; answering phones; buying groceries; reminding themselves they're important too.

GOSSIP COLUMNISTS

GOAL: Refer to heterosexual celebrity gaying it up all over the place without actually mentioning Clay Aiken by name.

ALLIES: Celebrities who need a little more buzz

ENEMIES: Celebrities who don't really want that buzz to be about sweatily grinding on the dance floor and falling down outside the club.

PROBLEM: Coming up with new superlatives to describe Jennifer Aniston when she talks to them, so they can do stories about how she'll never find true love.

REGRET: Asking Ashley Olsen to give you the *real* dirt on Mary-Kate. Who knew identical twins would stick together like that?

TRADE-OFF: Having to cover horseshit charity events for Darfur so they can have access to write about important things like celebrities' drug addictions and philandering.

TASK: Make new Kelly Clarkson album sound like a universe-changing development.

EXPERT ANALYSIS

Declined to comment: Bonnie Fuller, Janice Min

"Zac Efron has a little spring in his step after a hot and sweaty session at the gym Monday. Merrily he skips along! It's hard work maintaining that killer six pack. And we thank him for it!"

—Perez Hilton, from http://perezhilton.com

"Celebrity trumps everything, especially when 'everything' refers to Perez Hilton and the gang at *In Touch Weekly*. Look, I believe in the power of the press, but when you're up against second-fiddle coke-fiends with a God complex, one word of advice: Duck."

—Sarah Hepola, editor, www.salon.com

THE FIGHT

After scheduling a secret meeting to discuss the real reason behind their client's sudden "Vacation," the Celebrity Publicist and Celebrity Assistant still aren't there four hours later, causing the Paparazzi and Gossip Columnists to start panicking about deadlines, shoving each other, and frothing at the mouth. This devolves into an all-out brawl, when the Publicist and Assistant arrive with the world's best George Clooney and Leonardo DiCaprio impersonators, who begin making out with each other. There is a frenzied riot as everyone, completely fooled, tramples each other to take the first picture and break the story. By the time the Aniston and Jolie look-alikes finish having the lesbian sex, every member of the celebrity media has died a horrible, violent death.

THE WINNER

CELEBRITY PUBLICISTS AND CELEBRITY ASSISTANTS (KO)

ROBOT

ALLIES: Evil supercomputers; sinister vacuum cleaners

ENEMIES: Humanoids who created it and foolishly thought they could control it

GOAL: To take over the world slowly and insidiously

FAVORITE ARNOLD SCHWARZENEGGER ROLE: The Terminator

QUOTE: "I'll be back"— Terminator

CHARACTERISTIC: An electromagnetic system that appears to have sense and logic

FAVORITE MUSICIAN: Devo

FAVORITE TV SHOW: *Small Wonder*

EFFECT ON HUMAN THOUGHT: Makes us consider the true nature of intelligence.

IDEAL WOMAN: Daryl Hannah as an android in *Blade Runner*

DOMESTIC APPLICATION: Can perform simple but time-consuming household tasks like vacuum cleaning.

BARBARIAN

ALLIES: Frightened, tortured, captured people

ENEMIES: Will die, might be eaten.

GOAL: To take over the world by smashing it to death

FAVORITE ARNOLD SCHWARZENEGGER ROLE: Conan the Barbarian

QUOTE: "Crush your enemies, see them driven before you, hear the lamentations of their women."—Conan

CHARACTERISTIC: A human that appears to have no sense or logic

FAVORITE MUSICIAN: Ted Nugent

FAVORITE TV SHOW: *I Love the Middle Ages* (3D)

EFFECT ON HUMAN THOUGHT: Makes us consider how much we want to keep our fingers.

IDEAL WOMAN: Daryl Hannah as a Cro-Magnon in *Clan of the Cavebear*

TRAGIC HISTORY: Enslaved in ancient Greece

HOBBY: Plundering

ROBOT

TRAGIC HISTORY: Forced to star alongside Steve Guttenberg in *Short Circuit.*

HOBBY: Chess

DEFINITION: An automatically controlled, reprogrammable, multipurpose manipulator programmable in three or more axes

PEAK HISTORICAL PERIOD: The latter half of this century, when humans will be their slaves

THEY REPLACED: Assembly-line workers, and you're next if you don't step it up

BARBARIAN

DEFINITION: Guy you really don't want at your dinner party

PEAK HISTORICAL PERIOD: The Dark Ages

THEY REPLACED: Pretentious, arrogant Romans whose "art," "books," and "culture" couldn't save them

EXPERT ANALYSIS

"It's obvious this toothless Barbarian (no offense to those in Arkansas) is no match for the shiny, silicon-based, gear-wielding Robot. What the Robot lacks in attributes taken for granted by Mr. Barbarous, such as knee caps, tribal commitments, and the ability to make endless grunting noises, is easily made up for, and will no doubt be surpassed by, 360-degree joint rotations, wi-fi access to the mechanical repair wiki, and a vast inventory of high-pitched beeps and blonks. The only bit of advice I can offer the Robot is to watch out for the possible corrosive effects of the various gaseous discharges being emitted by his knuckle-dragging combatant."

—Roger Arrick, co-webmaster of http://robots.net and founder and president of Arrick Robotics

"The Barbarian would destroy any robot. The reasoning behind this is simple logic. Barbarians are invincible. Barbarians are cunning, deceptive, and masters of battle. They are not bound by any rules of morals, ethics, or fair war. They are willing to do whatever it takes to achieve victory. No robot could possibly stand a chance against such an awesome foe."

—Danny Soroudi, webmaster, the Official Barbaric Barbarians Webpage (www.rajuabju.com/barbarians)

"Physically, the Robot and Barbarian combatants are well matched—both are huge, heavily armed and well oiled. But the Barbarian's limited intellect cripples him in combat. The Robot will take advantage and strategically employ its giant buzz-saw hands to reduce the well-muscled human to a meaty spray of teeth, hair, and blood."

—Daniel Wilson, author of *How to Survive a Robot Uprising* and *How to Build a Robot Army*

THE FIGHT

The Robot, trained to sense human intelligence, begins to short-circuit when it notes the Barbarian is snacking on his own foot. The Barbarian takes advantage of this malfunction by clubbing the Robot repeatedly. The Robot beeps and points upward, and the Barbarian stares into the sun until he is blind. The Robot then slices through the Barbarian's stomach, ripping out his entrails and feeding them to him. The Barbarian enjoys his own entrails very much, but thinks they'd be even better with hot sauce.

THE WINNER

ROBOT (KO)

FLIRTING WITH DANGER FRAY

COQUETTE
VS.
COKEHEAD

COQUETTE

ALLIES: Guys who truly believe they've got a shot

ENEMIES: Those same guys at the end of the night, when they go home alone

TRADEMARK FIGHTING MOVE: The Free-Drink Penislock

WEAPONS: Eyes; lips; breasts; alcohol

POWER #1: She makes men lose all sense and decorum.

POWER #2: She can seemingly shrink space, so that a man believes her lightly touching his elbow in conversation is just one small step away from her spreading her legs in sweaty tribal junglesex.

POWER #3: She can make a hopeless romantic suddenly see a perfect magical future of love, hope, and beautiful babies, which is cruelly stolen from him by the better-looking, richer guy who just complimented her dress.

RECURRING PROBLEM #1: Men have no clue how to interpret body language, as we are fundamentally a wee bit stupid.

COKEHEAD

ALLIES: Cocaine dealers; dance club owners

ENEMIES: Employers; relatives

TRADEMARK FIGHTING MOVE: The Giant-Pupiled Deathchat

TRAVEL: Group field trips to bar bathrooms

CHARACTERISTICS: Sniffling nose; palpitating heart; miraculously efficient weight-loss program

BANK ACCOUNT: Dwindling due to some financial reprioritizing

PROBLEM #1: He's far less interesting than he believes.

PROBLEM #2: What goes up must come down.

PROBLEM #3: Oops, there goes his septum.

HIS OLD FRIEND: Can't keep up with his new and exciting lifestyle.

HIS NEW FRIEND: May or may not have just snorted kitty litter.

COQUETTE

RECURRING PROBLEM #2: Being called a whore for agreeing to converse with a man, but declining to have sexual intercourse with him.

MATH PROBLEM: Your purchase of two Cosmopolitans and one declaration that she's "really hot" equals:

a) One blow job
b) Fifteen minutes of conversation with a woman who'd otherwise give you fifteen seconds
c) Twenty dollars of misery

Answer below

THE FIGHT

The Coquette has just complimented the Cokehead on his shiny turquoise shirt when he overexcitedly rubs his nose a bit too hard, prompting a massive nosebleed. This necessitates an emergency trip to the men's room. And as long as he's in there . . .

THE WINNER

COQUETTE (TKO)

(Answer to Math Problem: C)

CLASH OF THE MUPPET COUPLES

KERMIT THE FROG AND MISS PIGGY
vs.

BERT AND ERNIE

KERMIT THE FROG AND MISS PIGGY

RESIDENCES: Swamps; fine hotels

FAVORITE PART OF THE HOUSE: Bedroom

ALLIES: Fozzie; Gonzo; the Swedish Chef; her fellow pigs in space; an endless array of guest stars like the great Mark Hamill

ENEMIES: The old guys in the balcony

FAVORITE TIME: Showtime

FAVORITE SEX ACT: Snout job

ROMANTIC PROBLEM: Kermit wants a "no-strings-attached" relationship (waka waka).

MAHNA-MAHNA?: Doo-doo-do-do-do

TRADEMARK FIGHTING MOVE: Karate Chop!

DOCTOR: Bunsen Honeydew

DESTINY: Worldwide superstardom

BERT AND ERNIE

RESIDENCE: Basement apartment on Sesame Street

FAVORITE PART OF THE HOUSE: The closet

ALLIES: Gay babies

ENEMIES: The Religious Right

FAVORITE TIME: Bathtime

FAVORITE SEX ACT: Peeling the ripe banana

BASEBALL PROBLEM: Two pitchers, no catcher

TRADEMARK FIGHTING MOVE: The Poopiefinger

DOCTOR: Will not accept joint coverage except in Massachusetts.

DESTINY: Unnatural acts with starstruck finger puppets

THE FIGHT

Kermit is strolling through New York's Tompkins Square Park at 2 A.M. following a Dr. Teeth and the Electric Mayhem show when Bert and Ernie ask him how much it would cost "just to pull your strings." Miss Piggy, who has been spying on her man, leaps out from behind a bush and beats the living crap out of the two gay Muppets. She then smacks Kermit around a little too, because he must have done something wrong.

THE WINNER

KERMIT AND MISS PIGGY (KO)

PIRATE

ALLY: His parrot

ENEMIES: Almost everybody else, including, often, his own shipmates

DOMAIN: Was rogue vessels, now generally hangs out on Ye Olde Internet.

BEST MOVIE: *Pirates of the Caribbean*, but only for the Keira Knightley factor

COOL GEAR: Eye patch; earring

SECRET WEAPON: A cornucopia of communicable venereal diseases

TRADEMARK FIGHTING MOVE: The Booty Snatcher (also his trademark sex move)

HISTORY: Dates back to the thirteenth century BCE, when yarrr actually meant something.

THE INTERNET: 42 percent of Web activity is devoted to who would win a fight between a pirate and ninja, with 37 percent devoted to porn and 21 percent to self-help (these are unofficial statistics).

NINJA

ALLIES: Shhhh, he's working.

ENEMIES: Could be anywhere.

DOMAIN: Your mother's bedroom, where he is hiding in her closet

BEST MOVIE: *Beverly Hills Ninja*, starring Chris Farley. This could be a matter of great debate, were I the type who gave a shit.

COOL GEAR: All-black outfits; split-toe boots ideal for silent wall climbing

SECRET WEAPON: Shall remain a secret until it kills you.

TRADEMARK FIGHTING MOVE: The Sword of Silence

HISTORY: Dates back to the Internet chat rooms of fourteenth-century feudal Japan.

THE INTERNET: Has been captured by stealthy adolescent ninjas with plastic throwing stars and embarrassing backne.

HOBBIES: Hiding in shadows; sabotage

PIRATE

HOBBIES: Plundering; looting; taking hostages; insulting ninja-lovers in Pirate vs. Ninja chat rooms

BEST YEARS: Mid-sixteenth to the mid-eighteenth centuries in the Caribbean

PERSONALITY: Rebel, rabble-rouser, doesn't play well with the other students

DANGER: Mutiny from his own crew and scurvy, which sounds cool but, trust me, is not.

FAMOUS PIRATES: Captain Morgan; Blackbeard

MOST POPULAR CURRENT SPOT FOR PIRATES BESIDES THE INTERNET: The Straits of Malacca in Indonesia, where the most pirate attacks occur

STRENGTH: Not constrained by typical morality.

WEAKNESS: Doesn't get around so well on his peg leg.

NINJA

BEST YEARS: The Kamakura–Edo Periods, and sophomore year, when he had like a hundred MySpace friends, including the cute girl from Science Camp.

PERSONALITY: Quiet, murderous

DANGER: Other silent Ninjas; being docked from the Internet by mean parents because of slipping grades

FAMOUS NINJAS: If a Ninja is famous, he is not doing his job properly.

MOST POPULAR CURRENT SPOT FOR NINJAS BESIDES THE INTERNET: Perched on your ceiling

STRENGTH: Extremely stealthy

WEAKNESS: Sometimes he's so good he can't find himself.

REASON FOR PIRATE VS. NINJA INTERNET PHENOMENON: See, pirates and ninjas are both cool but kind of opposite, see, because one's loud and the other . . . never mind.

EXPERT ANALYSIS

"I've always laughed at how much debate has surrounded this particular matchup because, to me, it seems extremely unbalanced. Let's take a look at the two competitors: On one side, you have these filthy, drunken peg-legged bastards who are more likely to vomit when opening their mouths than speak . . . on the other side, you have elite assassins who have dedicated their lives to mastering their deadly art and conditioning their bodies to endure levels of pain that would make most so-called 'tough guys' run for the hills at the mere mention of it. Don't get me wrong, I love pirates just as much as the next guy, but a single ninja could probably take out an entire pirate crew during their daily drunken slumbers. The ninja would cut off all the pirates' heads, load them into the ship's cannons and fire 'em off into the sea to celebrate his easy victory."

—Roger Barr, webmaster,
www.i-mockery.com

"Each human, if they were to look deeply into their own catacombs, would realize that there's pretty much no way a pirate could beat a ninja. It's preposterous. Here's why: First, a ninja is on a way higher maturity level than a pirate and wouldn't even bother, unless some pirate started talking major crap about the ninja and his amigos, which

is rude. And second, I'll scratch out the eyes of any man who disagrees with me on this subject. In conclusion, that might mean you, so chill."

—Robert Hamburger, ninja expert and author of *Real Ultimate Power: The Official Ninja Book* (www.realultimatepower.net)

"OMFG PIRATES HAVE GUNS!!! NO ONE CAN DODGE OR DEFLECT A BULLET SO DON'T EVEN SAY THAT YOU DUMB NINJA PUNKS PIRATES ARE SUPER!!!"

—Pirate voter,
www.piratevninja.com

"Dame it im a ninja but all of you ninjas are just talking about sex pirats are the ones that go around fucking bitchas not ninjas. Ninjas are honorable and can kill pirats eneywere and eneytime."

—Ninja voter,
www.piratevninja.com

"About 90 percent of the people voting for ninjas are just fans of Naruto or another stupid anime. These braindead people actually think that ninjas could reflect bullets with their swords and teleport and turn invisible. THEY CAN'T!!! Ninjas were just emo Asians who dressed in black pajamas and lived by a code, and killed themselves if they broke that code. Also: something to clear up about pirates: sure they drank, but not CONSTANTLY, also they could take the drinks like men unlike pussy ninjas."

—Pirate voter, www.piratevninja.com

"Ninjas can run around fuckin' bitches without the bitches even knowing they are being fucked. That's power. Ninja power."

—Ninja voter, www.piratevninja.com

THE FIGHT

Web servers all across the world are overloaded with predictions for this fight—and the match lives up to everyone's expectations, with sword fighting, explosions, and the expert dodging of throwing stars and bullets. The battle is earth-shattering, mind-blowing, orgasmic. The winner? I'll never tell.

THE WINNER

IT'S A SECRET, BITCHES.

METROSEXUAL

ALLIES: Homosexuals; women who fear bold, pure, unwiped masculinity

ENEMIES: Regular dudes now forced to buy product

FEARS: His clothing going out of style

FIGHTING ADVANTAGES: Capoeira training; well-toned physique

ADVANTAGE WITH WOMEN: Relates to and understands them

ANGERED BY: Poor aesthetics; hygiene

FAMOUS METROSEXUALS: David Beckham; Justin Timberlake; Pepé Le Pew

TWO THINGS HE DOES NOT HAVE: Pickup truck; fantasy football team

UNFORTUNATE CIRCUMSTANCE: Often mocked by men who lack style, grace, panache

ALSO KNOWN AS: Closeted homosexual

OFTEN FOUND IN: Barney's; Giorgio Armani; other men

FAVORITE TYPE OF NUT: Pignoli

EUNUCH

ALLIES: Weren't there in that moment of truth.

ENEMIES: Doctors who said he was having his appendix removed

FEARS: Nothing, as the worst has already happened.

FIGHTING ADVANTAGE: You can't kick him in the balls.

ADVANTAGE WITH WOMEN: He can't get them pregnant—not like they're sleeping with Billy No Balls anyway.

ANGERED BY: Everything makes him teste. (Hah! Sorry.)

FAMOUS EUNUCHS: Pierre Abelard; Judar Pasha; Morrissey

TWO THINGS HE DOES NOT HAVE: Guess

UNFORTUNATE CIRCUMSTANCE: Some asshole chopped off his balls.

ALSO KNOWN AS: Castrato

OFTEN FOUND IN: Royal courts; the opera

FAVORITE TYPE OF NUT: Cashew

FAVORITE TYPE OF BALL: Soccer

METROSEXUAL

FAVORITE TYPE OF BALL: Tennis

FAVORITE TYPE OF SACK: Knap

SPENDS TIME: Tying his ties; fixing his hair; shining his shoes

AS A BOY, HE: Played with dolls; loved to dance

MOISTURIZER: Three different types in the bathroom cabinet

DREAM: Someday he'll meet a woman as pretty as he is.

SEXUAL INTERCOURSE: Tantric

DON'T ASK HIM: About on-base percentage

FAVORITE SONG: "Fashion" by David Bowie

CHILDREN: Will not be constrained by traditional gender roles.

YOU MIGHT BE ONE IF: You've never discussed the size, shape, consistency of your feces.

EUNUCH

FAVORITE TYPE OF SACK: Gunny

SPENDS TIME: Trying not to cry

AS A BOY, HE: Had balls

MOISTURIZER: All of it in the world won't bring his balls back.

DREAM: Testicular transplant surgery

SEXUAL INTERCOURSE: Would be nice.

DON'T ASK HIM: To show you his balls

FAVORITE SONG: Anything by Michael Jackson

CHILDREN: Nope, got to have balls to make babies.

YOU MIGHT BE ONE IF: Someone just snuck up behind you and cut off your balls.

EXPERT ANALYSIS

"The advantage clearly goes to the Metrosexual in this contest. Plucked and waxed to aerodynamic perfection, the Metrosexual is not to be underestimated as his combination of higher testosterone levels, supreme self-awareness and a man-bag full of secret weapons makes him a potentially lethal opponent."

—Michael Flocker, author of
The Metrosexual Guide to Style
and *The Hedonism Handbook*

"There is a thriving underground circuit in Mexico where bastardized versions of this once-rich pageantry live on, and the Metrosexuals generally win, thanks to their exposure to magazines that reveal the secret to kick-ass abs and the like. But these death matches are by no means sanctioned bouts and are thus not an accurate bellwether for any sort of general forecasting."

—Peter Hyman, author of
The Reluctant Metrosexual

"Technically there is no distinction between a eunuch and a metrosexual. On one hand, you have a man with no penis, and on the other, you have a man with no penis with nice shoes. While the textbook definition of a eunuch is 'a man who has been castrated,' this definition lacks one important detail which may give a eunuch a slight edge over his sexually ambiguous counterpart: cause. If, for example, said eunuch lost his balls in a logging accident, then his virility cannot be questioned, and he may be so manly that a mere chodal remnant of his former sexuality could be enough to impregnate

a woman (possibly without physical contact)."

—Maddox, badass motherfucker,
www.alphabetofmanliness.com

"I don't understand why you would ask me this question. Hey, what are you doing with that ether and scissors?"

—My (former) friend Jon,
who should know better than
to call me during *The L Word*

THE FIGHT

The Metrosexual blinds the Eunuch with his hair spray and sticks nail clippers into his blinded eyes, leaving the Eunuch both eyeless and ball-less. It looks as though the castrato will be singing a tragic tune until, in his flailing, he manages to untuck the Metrosexual's shirt, which causes much shrieking and a fifteen-minute delay. Unfortunately, the Eunuch, by definition, cannot win, and he is unable to capitalize on this momentary advantage. When the Metrosexual is finally crisp again, he whacks the Eunuch with his man-bag, and then waxes and tans him completely while he's unconscious, adding insult to injury.

THE WINNER

METROSEXUAL (KO)

BAD REVIEW BATTLE
ARTIST
VS.
CRITIC
THOUGH HIS AGGRESSIVE BRUSHWORK MAY WIN HIM HUZZAHS FROM THE HOI POLLOI, I FOUND THE RESULT ULTIMATELY UNSATISFYING...

ARTIST

TOOLS: The imagination, both his own and that of other artists you've probably never heard of, or at least that's the gamble.

HOBBY: Analyzing his own work and figuring out his rightful place in the canon

LATEST PROJECT: Multimedia homage to George "The Animal" Steele

FUTURE PROJECT: Book without pages

PERFORMANCE ART PIECE: He watches you watching him watching you watching him.

LACKS: Health insurance; pension

REJECTS: Conventional definitions of beauty

LOVE INTEREST: Himself

WOMAN HE'S "DATING," ALTHOUGH THEY DON'T USE SUCH LIMITING, ANTIQUATED TERMS: Just made a finger painting of a baby with her own menstrual blood.

ALLIES: College students

ENEMIES: Other artists; critics

CRITIC

CHARACTERISTICS: Crotchety disposition; love of free stuff

MASTERPIECE: *Giving a Comic His Props: In Defense of Carrot Top*

FUNCTIONS: Arbiter of taste; crusher of dreams

FAVORITE WORDS: Pedantic; insipid; jejune

LOVE INTEREST: Didn't like being told their date "started promisingly but lapsed into trite clichés."

ALLIES: Artists with good reviews; people who want their culture prechewed before they eat it

ENEMIES: Artists with bad reviews

HIS OWN ART: Will never be shown to anyone. You know what critics are like?

HE LOVES: Work previously thought indecipherable, which he completely understands and will continue to explain at great length if you'll just come back here and stop shaking your head.

ARTIST

HIS EXPLANATION OF HIS WORK: Uses the phrase "negative space inextricably bonds the sacred to the profane."

CHARACTERISTICS: Provocateur; prolific lentil-eater

EXPERIMENTAL CROSS-DISCIPLINARY PRACTICE: Hiring a nude model in order to write a song.

TRADEMARK FIGHTING MOVE: The Aesthetic Armlock

VIEW ON HIGH AND LOW CULTURE: He believes there is no division between the two, as evidenced by his video installation in which *Scooby-Doo* episodes are edited so that Shaggy appears to be reciting T. S. Eliot's *The Waste Land.*

MASTERPIECE: Crucifixion mosaic composed entirely of cherry, lemon, and grape Nerds

CRITIC

CREATES: Animosity

LACKS: Creativity

REJECTS: The common misconceptions of the ignorant masses

TRADEMARK FIGHTING MOVE: Thumbs-down your eye socket

SECRET: Bought a blank canvas for $750,000 because he thought it was a white-on-white painting.

LATEST PROJECT: *Shakespeare, Shmakespeare: Why the Bard Was a Tard*

PROBLEM #1: Once he starts contextualizing, he can't stop.

PROBLEM #2: His editor will not allow him to describe contemporary artist Matthew Barney as a "big dumb pussyface."

PROBLEM #3: It's all been done before, and he sure as hell didn't do any of it.

EXPERT ANALYSIS

"Obviously Artists will kick the ass of Critics. But Critics will write a scathing review of the entire thing, give the Artists a meager two out of four stars, making clever use of the words 'pap' and 'pablum' before going home to their empty house and escalating drinking problem. And yet somehow, the Artists will be the ones in tears."

—Sarah Hepola, editor,
www.salon.com

"It's a battle of the assholes. Artist's head is lodged so far up his own asshole that the lightest tap in said region from Critic knocks him down fair-and-square. And we all know critics lerve to kick'em when they're down. Winner: Critic, hands down."

—Lisa Rosman, film critic, blogger,
The Broad View
(http://lisarosman.blogspot.com/)

"I'll have to give a small edge to Critic. For the most part, Critic vs. Artist will be a very nonphysical Jedi mind trick affair. Artist most definitely will draw blood early. But Critic has the size advantage and also sometimes knows what Artist is going to do before Artist does. So Artist goes for the kill early, but fails. Critic then makes him pay heavily with some 'you killed my brother, sister, momma, daddy, daughter, son, wife and potbellied pig' violence. When the dust settles, it won't be pretty. Critic may even be disfigured for life, but a win is a win and dead is dead."

—Chad Freeman, Las Vegas film critic and entertainment writer who runs the site www.pollystaffle.com

"This question is brilliant, and the rest of this book is a blinding light coming directly from God. I am overcome. I give it seven stars out of four."

—Acob Jay Alish Kay, the world's preeminent literary critic

THE FIGHT

The Artist's mode of attack is also his work, an indoor piece in which he and a thousand holograms of him all perform capoeira in drag to the sound of garbage trucks loading and unloading refuse as marshmallows fall from the ceiling. The Critic characterizes this as "lazily conceived and embarrassingly unoriginal," and opens a giant trapdoor, which the Artist and his holograms fall through.

THE WINNER

CRITIC (KO)

FIGHTS

BECAUSE I SAID SO

★ I'M WRITING THIS BOOK
AND YOU'RE NOT,
SO SUCK IT

MAGIC SWORD BATTLE
HE-MAN
VS.
SHE-MALES

HE-MAN

ORIGINALLY: A 1981 Mattel action figure, with twist waist and "power punch action"

CIVILIAN IDENTITY: Prince Adam

OCCUPATION: Master of the Universe

BASE OF OPERATIONS: Eternia

CHARACTERISTICS: Bulging muscles; itsy-bitsy shorts; girlish haircut; love for his cat

IDENTITY/CLASS: Human transformed by magic

POWERS/ABILITIES: Able to transform himself into He-Man by drawing the Sword of Power and invoking the phrase "By the Power of Grayskull, I have the Power," which could be shortened to "I have the Power of Grayskull." Poor editing. Can also change his scaredy-cat Cringer into the ferocious steed Battlecat.

ALLIES: She-Ra; Sorceress; Ram Man; Fisto (Really. Ram Man and Fisto)

SHE-MALES*

ORIGINALLY: A dude

CIVILIAN IDENTITY: Once Lou, now Lola

OCCUPATION: Porn star; prostitute; person at work you can't look in the eyes

BASE OF OPERATIONS: New York's West Side Highway; Hollywood Boulevard; "Boys Town" In Nuevo Laredo, Mexico

CHARACTERISTICS: Large hands; deep voice; itsy-bitsy shorts; feminine haircut; constant misuse of the words "she" and "woman"

IDENTITY/CLASS: Human transformed by hormones

POWERS/ABILITIES: Able to convince a "totally straight" man that masturbating to/ having sex with someone with a penis "isn't gay at all," or even that the dick in his mouth is attached to "a beautiful woman."

ALLIES: Any man looking to save money on his hooker

*Obviously, a battle between the superpowered He-Man and a single She-Male is unfair. Similarly, asking He-Man to take on all who self-identify as female-to-male transsexuals is patently absurd. So this battle is between He-Man and ten She-Males, in order to be realistic.

HE-MAN

ENEMIES: Skeletor; Beast Man; Whiplash; Flogg

WEAPON: Sword of Power, used to overwhelm enemies; Axe and Shield, for overkill

POTENTIAL WEAKNESSES: Tendency to misplace Sword; power outage in Grayskull

FEARS: Skeletor's deadly Havok Staff; hanging brain out of tiny fur shorts during battle

SHE-MALES

ENEMIES: Religious people; squares who think "women" have to have "vaginas"

WEAPON: Sword of Power, used to shock the drunk, unobservant

POTENTIAL WEAKNESSES: Tendency to absentmindedly forget to shave face and/or chest; inability to locate size-13 high heels

FEARS: Having "the conversation"; hanging brain out of bikini bottoms while on beach

EXPERT ANALYSIS

Declined to comment: He-Man

"Once he has transformed from Adam, He-Man has the power of Grayskull within. So he could easily handle ten regular humans, regardless of sex and emotional state."

—Webmaster, www.heman.org, the #1 He-Man fan site

"I don't know what you're talking about, honey. Do you want a good time or not?"

—Annie, transsexual prostitute

THE FIGHT

Though Prince Adam summons the Power of Grayskull when he sees the strangely broad-shouldered females approaching, he is unprepared when one casually reaches into his tiny fur shorts and quotes him an extremely reasonable price. Before he knows it he is lying naked, confused, and scared on plastic sheets in a Mexican border town, ten she-swords poking at his He-Mangina.

THE WINNER

SHE-MALES (SUBMISSION)

NECROPHILIAC

ALLIES: Really flying solo with this one, unlikely to find much support

ENEMIES: Pretty much the whole civilized world

QUESTION #1: Whom is he hurting, you know, *really*?

QUESTION #2: What if he'd also had sex with the person when they were alive? Then it's kind of consensual, right? Right?

QUESTION #3: Shouldn't he perhaps be seen as a sexual adventurer, an explorer of undiscovered orifices?

PROBLEM #1: Sexual partners tend to be fairly unresponsive.

PROBLEM #2: He has to find the fresh ones, as decay can be a turnoff.

PROBLEM #3: It's a lot to explain when you're caught.

ANCIENT CULTURES: Used necrophilia as a means of communicating with the dead, which makes just as much sense as mediums and is a whole lot more bang for your buck.

GHOST OF THE DEAD WOMAN HE'S SCREWING

ALLIES: Fellow ghosts, who were hoping for a less filthy eternity

ENEMY: Civil liberties lawyer ghost, who's just being difficult

QUESTION #1: *Why?* Dear God, *Why?*

QUESTION #2: Couldn't you have at least brought flowers?

QUESTION #3: Can you put my eyeball back in now?

PROBLEM #1: This guy is totally not my type, mostly because he has sex with dead people.

PROBLEM #2: I'm *so* embarrassed by how I look, what with my skin rotting off my bones.

PROBLEM #3: You didn't wear a condom, and now I'm pregnant with an evil demon spawn. Thanks, Pervy Pervenberg. Your town's fucked.

THE FIGHT

The Necrophiliac is in the midst of something extremely experimental with the corpse's ear canal when the Ghost happens upon him. Repulsed (and yes, a bit intrigued), she kicks him and her corpse back into the grave and, with speed only the dead can summon, shovels dirt on the lovers, who are still conjoined. The next necrophiliac who comes by is in for a hell of a surprise.

THE WINNER

GHOST OF THE DEAD WOMAN HE'S SCREWING (KO)

BATTLE OF THE NOBLE WARRIORS

SAMURAI

vs.

GLADIATOR

SAMURAI

CLASS: Military nobility

JOB: Sword-wielding lord's servant

WEAPONS: Enviably large kitana sword; cool armor

SKILLS: Archery; fencing; ability to make words come out a split second before or after lips move, confusing enemies

GUIDING PRINCIPLE: Bushido, the code of ethics

HOBBIES: Calligraphy; haiku; perfecting karaoke version of "Tainted Love"

ALLIES: Emperors; geishas; their horses

ENEMIES: Raging Mongols; marauding bandits; crippling peer pressure; Americans who bring atomic bombs to swordfights

LOVE INTEREST: Girl with pink hair and many bracelets who giggles indiscriminately

FAVORITE TV SHOW: Involves laughing at people on the toilet, dancing girls, and a singing lizard

GLADIATOR

CLASS: Differed between slaves, prisoners of war, and volunteers

JOB: Showbiz

WEAPONS: Sword; whip; shield; bad attitude

SKILL: Able to titillate future generations with their sandals and leather wear.

GUIDING PRINCIPLE: Try not to die.

HOBBIES: Complex mathematics; taking down Philip Morris

ALLIES: Yes, please.

ENEMIES: Each other; condemned criminals; wild animals

LOVE INTEREST: Digs him, but bet on the lion.

LEAD-IN: *Public Execution Live! with Regis and Kelly*

CHARACTERISTICS: Focused; ferocious; a little pissed about his profession's 97 percent mortality rate

TIME PERIOD: Third century B.C. to the fifth century A.D.

SAMURAI

WEAKNESS: Tendency to commit ritual suicide when disheartened

SECRET WEAPON: $3/4$-inch cell phone/MP3 player/video camera/computer/sushi knife/robot/sex toy/grenade

TIME PERIOD: Seventh to nineteenth centuries

RELIGION: Mostly Buddhist, except for one overacting Scientologist

GAY PRACTICE: Shudo, or love between a seasoned and novice Samurai. Really.

RELAXATION: Zen meditation

RELATIONSHIP TO SWORD: Considered his kitana his soul and gave it a name, a precursor to the twenty-first-century man's relationship to his penis.

PAY: Measured in rice. Not kidding.

FAVORITE WORD: *Tsujigiri,* Japanese for testing out one's sword on a passerby. I swear.

GLADIATOR

RELIGION: Involves very specific, rapid, intense prayer

GAY PRACTICE: Just that once at Caligula's afterparty

RELAXATION: Moment of peace after the chains are removed and before the lion attacks

RELATIONSHIP TO SWORD: Really fond of not being stabbed with one

CONTRACT: They swore an oath to give their lives to Gods of the Underworld and accept any and all humiliation—which, if you think about it, is a pretty shitty oath.

EXPERT ANALYSIS

"The bash and slash style of the heavy westerners was an appropriate technique for the Gladiators. Their sword was to be used in conjunction with other instruments like another sword, a net, shield, or trident. Though this could pose some difficulty for Samurai, their approach to the intricacies of Japanese-style fencing and the precision details of technique and strategy would win the day for the Samurai."

—Russell McCartney, seventh-degree black belt; sword master; holder of the Guinness world record for target cutting with a sword; founder of the United States Sword Foundation

"The fighting skills needed by a Gladiator were very different from those needed by a Samurai; the same was true of his equipment. His armor was highly ornamented and not designed to protect the man from serious injury. The rules governing Gladiator fights were strictly enforced by a referee. Victory and cash rewards—which could be huge—were awarded on the basis of skill and popularity. In contrast the Samurai were warriors who fought in battles. Their armor was designed to minimize life-threatening injuries to head and body. If combat were fought according to strict Gladiator rules then the Gladiator would

have the edge, but in a free fight the Samurai would probably come out on top."

—Rupert Matthews, author, *100 Gladiators* and *The Age of the Gladiators: Savagery and Spectacle in Ancient Rome*

THE FIGHT

Samurai and Gladiator engage in a complex, artful, epic dance of death that sees each man seemingly get the upper hand, before being repelled by acts of pure combat mastery. After two hours, a bored Emperor releases a pack of wild lions on the Gladiator, who is torn limb from limb. Ashamed by his hollow victory, the Samurai draws his kitana and commits ritual seppuku. The lion eats them both, and the Emperor switches the channel to *America's Got Talent.*

THE WINNER

SAMURAI (KO)

MICHAEL CORLEONE

ALIAS: Godfather

OCCUPATION: Godfather

HERITAGE: Sicilian

BASE OF OPERATIONS: New York

IDOLIZED BY: Two-bit mobsters; film aficionados

ENEMIES: Some Italian-American groups; anyone who saw *Godfather III*

CHARACTERISTICS: Contemplative stare; thirst for power

OBSERVATIONAL SKILLS: Highly attuned

BEFORE HE WAS A BIG-TIME VIOLENT CRIMINAL, HE: Was an Ivy Leaguer and World War II hero.

AS HE GAINS POWER, HE: Loses love.

IF THERE WERE A TOWER OF FILM, HE'D: Reside in a penthouse apartment.

MURDERS: Usually carried out by others, in secret.

HOT WASPY LOVE INTEREST: Kay Adams (Diane Keaton)

TONY MONTANA

ALIAS: Scarface

OCCUPATION: Yeyo dealer

HERITAGE: Cuban

BASE OF OPERATIONS: Miami

IDOLIZED BY: Two-bit gangstas; the hip-hop community

ENEMIES: Cuban-Americans; film critics

CHARACTERISTICS: Constant use of the word "fuck"; thirst for power

OBSERVATIONAL SKILLS: Minimal

BEFORE HE WAS A BIG-TIME VIOLENT CRIMINAL, HE: Was a small-time violent criminal.

AS HE GAINS POWER, HE: Gains cocaine.

IF THERE WERE A TOWER OF FILM, HE'D: Have a dingy, coke-strewn one-bedroom, and often wake up his neighbors by shooting at his television.

MURDERS: Carried out by himself, publicly.

GODFATHER

POPULAR AND PROFOUNDLY VIOLENT VIDEO GAME?: Absolutely

MEMORABLE QUOTE: "Keep your friends close and your enemies closer."

TRAGIC FLAW: Inability to avoid his fate

VALUABLE LESSON: You can't escape your family.

SCARFACE

HOT WASPY LOVE INTEREST: Elvira Hancock (Michelle Pfeiffer)

POPULAR AND PROFOUNDLY VIOLENT VIDEO GAME?: For sure

MEMORABLE QUOTE: "Say hello to my little friend!"

TRAGIC FLAW: Overacting

VALUABLE LESSON: Don't get high on your own supply.

EXPERT ANALYSIS

"If it was a battle of organizations— Michael would kick the low-rent Tony Montana's ass up around his ears. But mano a mano? Michael is a silver-spooned mafioso. Montana would distract Michael with a coke cloud and a fucking grenade launcher down the throat. Tony would make Michael his bitch!"

—Harry Knowles, film critic for *Penthouse*, founder of the renowned film site www.aintitcool.com

"Tony Montana would win because Tony didn't grow up in the lap of luxury. Michael and his brothers were tough, but I bet the Cuban barrio was tougher than what kids of a mob boss had to deal with. Montana didn't do the Ivy League like Corleone—although Michael was one ruthless SOB. However, round for round, pound for pound, I'd have my money on the man who already had a hole in his belly from hunger and a scar on his face."

—L. A. Banks, author of *Scarface, Volume 1* and *Scarface, Point of No Return*

"Is this really a fair fight? Because when we say Tony Montana versus Michael Corleone, we're really talking mid-career Pacino, deep in the booze and his own mythology, versus early-career Pacino, still young and full of cum but never dumb. Michael may lack Tony's coked-up bluster, but he mans both U.S. coasts with a cool-headed strategy that bodes well for the ring. And, let's face it: All Corleone has to do is land one square on Tony's nose and the resulting nosebleed will stop time. Conclusion: Corleone, duh."

—Lisa Rosman, film critic, blogger, The Broad View (http://lisarosman.blogspot.com)

THE FIGHT

Corleone and Montana meet at an Italian restaurant to discuss a multi-million-dollar cocaine deal. After both men are searched for weapons, Montana, between frequent trips to the bathroom, animatedly discusses the joys of "fucking yeyo, fucking murder, and just plain fucking" and introduces Michael to his "little friend" and contact, Pedro the drug-dealing dwarf. Michael excuses himself to the bathroom to sample the product, where he retrieves a gun Clemenzo has secured for him, murders Scarface, and leaves with the drugs and the dwarf.

THE WINNER

MICHAEL CORLEONE (KO)

SCIENTIST

ALLIES: Mathematicians; doctors; philosophers; engineers

ENEMIES: Religious crazies; anyone who failed advanced bio or physics

IS: That kid who was so much smarter than you that he just had to have a wedgie.

BELIEF: That a combination of hypothesis, empirical evidence, and experimentation yields advancement, and that our understanding of the world is constantly developing.

ALIASES: Nerd; loser

HEROES: Einstein; Newton; Darwin

POWERS AND ABILITIES: Able to explain the seemingly inexplicable, grant the eyes of knowledge to blind faith.

SEX SYMBOL: Marie Curie, but just because she's the only woman

FAVORITE FILM: *Microcosmos*

THEORY ON MAN'S CREATION: Humans co-evolved with apes from a common ancestor.

SCIENTOLOGIST

ALLIES: Batshit crazy people; apeshit crazy people; various other loons

ENEMIES: The sane

IS: A rich and powerful actor or musician who believes he or she needs more freedom and preferential treatment. That, or just a regular crazy person.

BELIEF: In aliens, but not psychiatry or prescription medication

ALIASES: Tom Cruise; John Travolta

HERO: L. Ron Hubbard, a crappy sci-fi writer

POWERS AND ABILITIES: The highest-level OT, or Operating Thetan (which Tom Cruise is believed to be), is an enlightened being who can move inanimate objects with his mind, leave his body, and telepathically communicate with humans and animals. Not kidding.

SEX SYMBOLS: Katie Holmes; Dharma; the wife from *King of Queens*

FAVORITE FILM: *Battlefield Earth*

SCIENTIST

NOTABLE ACCOMPLISHMENTS:
Discoveries of atoms, genes,
gravity

OTHER PLANETS: Provide invaluable
information about Earth and
our universe.

THE SECRETS OF OUR UNIVERSE: Will
never be fully comprehended,
which does not mean the effort
isn't worthy.

IMMORTALITY: Nope

PRIZE: Nobel

METHODS: Research; observation;
experimentation

JOURNALISTS: Report on
significant scientific
advancement.

HOMOSEXUALITY: Occurs in a
number of species, including
penguins and sheep.

BRAIN: Expanding

SCIENTOLOGIST

THEORY ON MAN'S CREATION:
Seventy-five million years ago,
Xenu brought billions of people
to earth in his spacecraft, put
them by volcanoes, and blew
them up with H-bombs. Their
souls, or "Body Thetans," stick
to the bodies of the living,
causing harm. Still not kidding.

NOTABLE ACCOMPLISHMENTS: *Grease;*
Top Gun

OTHER PLANETS: Are where we
lived our past lives.

THE SECRETS OF OUR UNIVERSE: Can
be yours for enough money.

IMMORTALITY: We are all immortal
Thetans who have lived trillions
of years.

PRIZE: A five-picture deal

METHODS: Auditing, in which a
small current is passed through
tin cans you are holding and
changes in electrical resistance
are measured. This rehabilitates
your spirit.

JOURNALISTS: Are banned from
being Scientologists.

HOMOSEXUALITY: Can be prayed
and paid away.

BRAIN: Washing

EXPERT ANALYSIS

Declined to comment: Xenu

"The Scientist would beat the Scientologist, because—over the long term—science is beating everything (with the possible exception of the mass media)."

—Bruce Charlton, editor of
Medical Hypotheses magazine,
author of *The Modernization
Imperative,* and champion of
the theory of psychological
neoteny, which states that
it is advantageous in both science
and modern life to have a
personality type characterized
by prolonged youthfulness

"Simply unfair. While the Scientist would be plotting out the most logical and systematic way to attack his enemy, the Scientologist would distract the Scientist by jumping up and down on a couch like a retard while they take away the Scientist's power of logic. As the Scientist stares in awe, five L. Ron Hubbard lawyers would flank the Scientist. Allegedly. Easiest win in the whole book: Scientology."

—Keith and the Girl, hosts of the free
comedy show and podcast found at
www.keithandthegirl.com

"We are just an advanced breed of monkeys on a minor planet of a very average star. But we can understand the universe. That makes us something very special."

—Stephen Hawking

"Two things are infinite: the universe and human stupidity; and I'm not sure about the universe."

—Albert Einstein

"The first principle is that you must not fool yourself—and you are the easiest person to fool."

—Richard Feynman

"Some people, well, if they don't like Scientology, well, then, fuck you. Really. Fuck you. Period."

—Tom Cruise, in *Rolling Stone* magazine

THE FIGHT

Preferring not to fight but prepared for any possible eventuality, the Scientist brings both a copy of Stephen Hawking's *A Brief History of Time* and a machine gun. He is attempting to explain the Big Bang Theory to the creepily chipper Scientologist when Xenu comes down in his spacecraft and blows him up with an H-bomb.

THE WINNER

SCIENTOLOGIST (KO)

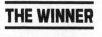

DISTURBING PURPLE
CREATURES QUARREL

BARNEY
<u>VS.</u>
GRIMACE

BARNEY

CHARACTERISTICS: Purple anthropomorphic T-Rex

DEMEANOR: Friendly and cheerful

ALLIES: Preschool kids

ENEMIES: Parents who have to pretend to like this horseshit

LOVES: Singing

LOVE INTEREST: The gay Teletubby

MONOSYLLABIC UTTERANCE: Yay

LITTLE-KNOWN FACT: He funny-touches preschoolers.

SAD TRUTH: He's perfectly age-appropriate, which means three-year-olds are retarded.

GRIMACE

CHARACTERISTICS: Purple anthropomorphic big blobby thing

DEMEANOR: Dumb and loyal

ALLY: Ronald McDonald, who would never make unhealthy food for the beautiful little boys and girls

ENEMIES: The Hamburgler; wildly unpopular organic-food characters Baby Carrot and Ricky Rice Cakes

LOVES: Milk shakes

LOVE INTERESTS: Unrequited love for Cookie Puss and Fudgie the Whale

MONOSYLLABIC UTTERANCE: Duh

LITTLE-KNOWN FACT: The McRib was made from his Uncle O'Grimacey.

SAD TRUTH: Not even he knows what goes in those McNuggets.

THE FIGHT

This battle is fought in court, where Barney's lawyers allege on behalf of parents that Grimace and his McDonald's cohorts have made American children fat, while Grimace's attorneys make the counterclaim, also for parents, that Barney has made American children dumb. The judge decides they're both right, and awards everyone billions of dollars, which we immediately waste on lottery tickets.

THE WINNER

A DRAW BETWEEN FATNESS AND STUPIDITY

RESEARCH GRANT RUMBLE

INSIGNIFICANT ACADEMIC
VS.
LESS SIGNIFICANT ACADEMIC RIVAL

INSIGNIFICANT ACADEMIC

ALLY: The head of the department, who thinks he's a genius

ENEMY: Less Significant Academic Rival, who he believes may have defecated on his doorstep

GOAL: The feature article in an obscure and unreadable academic journal

PROBLEM: No one has ever done this with the semicolon before.

HIS BOOK: Is sold in the campus bookstore, and taught in his friends' graduate courses.

CHALLENGE #1: Figuring out how to boot opond his grant money

CHALLENGE #2: Going against academia's conventional wisdom on the parentheses without alienating or insulting his colleagues, who must referee his peer review.

TRADEMARK FIGHTING MOVE: Thesis to the Throat

MISTAKE: Attributing a quote to Bloomfield that was actually uttered by Chomsky.

LESS SIGNIFICANT ACADEMIC RIVAL

ALLY: His girlfriend, who thinks he's kind of smart when he isn't trying too hard

ENEMY: Insignificant Academic, who was out of town presenting at a major conference when he cleverly defecated on his doorstep

GOAL: Any article in an obscure, unreadable academic journal

PROBLEM: "Suck it" is not a legitimate critique of a dissertation.

HIS BOOK: Was clearly self-published, as "Misunderstood Genius Books" is not a real publisher.

CHALLENGE #1: Figuring out whom he can safely plagiarize.

CHALLENGE #2: Getting tenure without doing anything at all of merit.

TRADEMARK FIGHTING MOVE: The Comparative Analysis Crescent Kick

MISTAKE: Attributing many quotes to Schmendelbrot, whom he completely made up.

THE FIGHT

Insignificant Academic, furious with Less Significant Academic Rival's assessment of his book as a "towering pillar of mediocrity" in a recently published review, beats his less significant rival over the head with his book and slaps him senseless with his doctorate degree. Less Significant Academic Rival tries to hit Insignificant Academic with his prized Third Place Dissertation plaque from the Myrtle Beach Linguistics Conference and Mini Golf Getaway, but, like respect and glory, it falls out of his grasp. Insignificant Academic is about to shove an academic journal down Less Significant Academic Rival's esophagus when Less Significant Academic Rival cries uncle, packs up his things, and returns to his small hometown to teach ninth-grade English and coach the debate team.

THE WINNER

INSIGNIFICANT ACADEMIC (TKO)

NAKED MOLE RAT

ORDER: Rodentia (burrowing rodent)

GENUS: *Heterocephalus*

TRAITS: Lack of pain sensation in skin; cold-blooded metabolism

ADAPTATIONS: Can move backward as fast as forward, with huge protruding teeth it uses to dig.

NATIVE TO: The drier parts of tropical grasslands of East Africa, where it lives underground in tunnels it digs with its giant protruding teeth.

SOCIAL STRUCTURE: Only the queen mole rat reproduces, with one to three males, while the rest of the mole rats function as a colony of workers, similar to ants or termites.

REASON FOR INFERTILITY IN FEMALES: Temporary reproductive suppression

FUN FACT: Their skin lacks the neurotransmitter Substance P, which sends pain signals to the central nervous system.

ALLIES: Each other, as clusters of seventy-five to eighty live and work together.

MOLE RAT IN FORMAL WEAR

ORDER: *Rodentia elegantia* (burrowing rodent with impeccable style)

GENUS: *Metrocephalus*

TRAITS: Tastes for the finest wines, clothes, women

ADAPTATIONS: Silky smooth in any social situation

NATIVE TO: The galleries of Manhattan; the cafés of Paris; the casinos of Monte Carlo; the most luxurious hotels the world has to offer

SOCIAL STRUCTURE: Often hosts the wildest pool parties, where lovely ladies lounge topless by the grotto.

REASON FOR INFERTILITY IN FEMALES: He does not drill without the pill, as a baby would cramp his style.

FUN FACT: Every woman blessed by his touch has experienced multiple orgasms.

ALLIES: Perhaps you've heard of Martin Scorsese? How about a little actor by the name of George Clooney?

NAKED MOLE RAT

ENEMIES: Rufous-beaked snakes

ALSO KNOWN AS: Sand puppy; desert mole rat

DIET: Large tubers; own feces

MOLE RAT IN FORMAL WEAR

ENEMIES: Jealous mole rats who lack confidence and style

ALSO KNOWN AS: Romeo; El Rey de la Corazon

DIET: Lobster; caviar; own feces

THE FIGHT

The Naked Mole Rat ("NMR") burrows through Beverly Hills and emerges in the Mole Rat in Formal Wear's ("MRIFW") bedroom, where he is in his silk robe entertaining his "Three Jessicas"—Alba, Simpson, and Biel. The horrified starlets immediately throw on their underthings and scamper away. The NMR shows the MRIFW his birth certificate, which shows they're brothers separated since birth. The MRIFW has his bodyguards beat the NMR with sticks until he crawls off, bloody and distraught. Then, overcome with guilt, the MRIFW chases down the NMR and hands him some books on etiquette and an ascot.

THE WINNER

MOLE RAT IN FORMAL WEAR (KO)

HAN SOLO

TIME: Long ago in a galaxy far, far away

ALLIES: Chewbacca; Luke Skywalker; two generations of maladjusted adolescents

ENEMIES: Darth Vader; Jabba the Hutt

LOVE INTERESTS: Princess Leia; Ally McBeal

LOW POINT: Being frozen in carbonite

HIGH POINT: Destroying the Death Star

SUPERPOWER: More than any man in the world, Harrison Ford's presence makes the most jaded, blasé New York hipster into an awestruck eight-year-old.

GREATEST ACCOMPLISHMENT: Able to make horrid *Star Wars* dialogue actually sound pretty damn good.

INCREDIBLY COOL LESSER-KNOWN ACQUAINTANCES: Rick Deckard and the Replicants

INDIANA JONES

TIME: From 1936 until Harrison Ford drops dead

ALLIES: Ready to betray him at a moment's notice

ENEMIES: Nazis; boulders

LOVE INTEREST: Hard-drinking crazy woman Marion Ravenwood, who gets captured like five times in *Raiders*

GOAL: Retrieve the Ark of the Covenant

ORIGINALLY CAST: Tom Selleck

FEAR: Snakes

SKILLS: World's greatest archaeologist; speaks twenty-seven languages

EXTREMELY COOL JOHN WILLIAMS THEME THAT EVERY KID IN ELEMENTARY SCHOOL RAN AROUND THE PLAYGROUND SINGING WHILE PRETENDING TO WHIP ME: "Da-ta-da-ta-da-ta-daaaa"

DUMB ELEMENTARY SCHOOL INDIANA JONES JOKE: "Hey, hey! *My* staff is too long!"

HAN SOLO

GOOFY SIDEKICK: Chewbacca

VIDEO GAMES: Yes, many

OCCUPATION: Smuggler; Reluctant Hero; Slickest Cat in the Universe thirty years running

PERSONALITY: Reckless, cynical loner; closet idealist

SKILLS: Expert pilot with quick-draw ability and amazing sense for impending danger

CRUEL INEVITABILITY: No matter what I write about *Star Wars*, some loser who's seen the movie 179 times will correct me.

INDIANA JONES

PROBLEM #1: Lots of really disappointed archaeology majors in college who expected bullwhips and radios for speaking to God.

PROBLEM #2: It's easy to teach the monkey to heil Hitler; it's hard to make it stop heiling Hitler when company's at the house.

WEAPONS: Wit; whip

GOOFY SIDEKICK: Short Round

TRADEMARK FIGHTING MOVE: Bringing a gun to a knife fight

VIDEO GAMES: Of course

OCCUPATION: Professor of archaeology; badass

INSPIRATION: Among others, Percy Harrison Fawcett, a British archaeologist who went into the Amazon jungle in 1925 in search of a lost city and never reappeared

EXPERT ANALYSIS

"It depends on whether it's original-version Han or Special Edition Han—because to beat Indy, Han better shoot first!"

—Evan "Rainbow Droideka" Centanni,
webmaster of the
www.yodasdatapad.com
Star Wars site

"Always something of a reluctant fighter, it's difficult to see how Solo's skills with technology would help him here. Jones's academic background hasn't stopped him from learning how to handle a bullwhip and he would soon be using it to separate Solo from his blaster, leaving him wide open to the physical prowess of the adventurer."

—Graham Thompson, author of
American Culture in the 1980s

"In a Han Solo vs. Indiana Jones fight, aoouming that it io only botwccn thooc two and they don't bring in Chewbacca or Sallah or whoever, it seems that Indy would have the upper hand, as he is a bit more skilled in survival than Han. Indy has used his survival skills and quick instinct to get himself out of many sticky situations, while Han seems to rely on others. Han holds the philosophy that all he needs is his blaster and his wit."

—Adamwankenobi (aka Adam Kingrey),
frequent contributor to www.

Wookieepedia.org (the *Star Wars* wiki) and various other *Star Wars* sites

THE FIGHT

Off on a remarkably well-funded archaeological expedition to Tatooine to find the remains of a mythical gargantuan creature called Jabba the Hutt, Indiana encounters Solo, who is guzzling Colt '45s on a stoop with Lando Calrissian, bemoaning the fact they've been out of work for a quarter-century while dipshits like Jar Jar Binks make bank off the *Star Wars* franchise. Indy feels terrible for his downtrodden doppelgänger, hands him a roll of bills from the new *Indiana Jones* profits, and places a call to the intergalactic drunk tank. Solo doesn't want his pity, breaks his malt-liquor bottle over his head, and stabs him with the broken bottle until a swarm of Wookies restrains him.

THE WINNER

HAN SOLO (KO)

SMALL MAN WITH BREASTS

ALLIES: Blackout drunks of either gender who manage to find *something* they like

ENEMIES: Men who insult him but kind of want to cop a feel

STRENGTH: Has more to work with than your average masturbator.

WEAKNESS: Well, he's a tiny dude with tits.

SAD TRUTH #1: At the beach, he has to wear a one-piece that kind of makes him look like a littler Ethel Merman.

SAD TRUTH #2: High-school bullies got a little aroused by giving him titty twisters.

SCIENTIFIC NAME FOR CONDITION: Gynecomastia

SCIENTIFIC PROCESS: Testosterone the liver can't process converts to estrogen.

CAUSES OF HIS CONDITION: Puberty and antidepressants, which don't make a fella less depressed if they give him breasts.

LARGE BALDING WOMAN

ALLIES: Extremely drunk men; average-looking women who are comparatively gorgeous

ENEMY: Herself

STRENGTH: Appreciates whatever she gets.

WEAKNESS: Kind of looks like Young Frankenstein.

CARPET: Matches the drapes, but is much hairier.

MUST-HAVE ACCESSORIES: Wig; lipstick; bottle of liquor; handgun for when she finally concludes the first three will never work

SECRET HOPE: That just once she'll be objectified.

SAD TRUTH #1: There isn't even a fetish for her, and there are fetishes for everything.

SAD TRUTH #2: She's not even feminine for a tranny.

SAD TRUTH #3: You can't look at her and you can't look away.

SMALL MAN WITH BREASTS

OCCUPATION: Telemarketer

NICKNAME: Sugar Tits

SURGERY: Going in for the breast reduction, but might spring for the penis enlargement.

COMFORTING STATISTIC: A mild form of gynecomastia affects up to 70 percent of pubescent boys, although almost all of them grow out of it, unlike Knockers McGee over there.

TRADEMARK FIGHTING MOVE: The Boobie Trap

OVERCOMPENSATING MOVES: He smokes cigars, plays poker, beats up smaller men with bigger breasts.

DOESN'T: Take his shirt off in public.

DOES: Wear a sports bra while watching sporting events.

LARGE BALDING WOMAN

TRIP TO THE HAIRSTYLIST: Asked for the Rachel, got the Jeff Van Gundy.

NICKNAME: Dr. Phil, which is so not fair, because her mustache is thinner.

OCCUPATION: Was an overnight cleaning lady; became a nurse in the terminal ward.

OPTIONS: Shave head; slouch; diet; blind herself with a sharp stick

TRADEMARK FIGHTING MOVE: The Kiss of Horror

HAIRS ON HEAD: 633 at the start of this sentence, 632 now

CHARACTERISTICS: Has lots of caps, shame.

LOVE INTEREST: Her right hand, which isn't attracted to her either.

PERSONALITY: Introverted, which is how everyone likes it.

MAJOR EXPENSE: Female hair-loss products, which just make her a poor balding woman.

WINS: Two championships in college as a field hockey goalie

LARGE BALDING WOMAN

LOSSES: 79 hairs a day

CAUSE OF HER CONDITION: Her hair follicles are attacked by her own immune system, which is a dick.

COMFORTING STATISTIC: Half of all women are affected by some hair loss by age fifty, although those women also point at her and whisper.

EXPERT ANALYSIS

Declined to comment: Large Balding Woman, Small Man with Breasts

"For some men like me, it's a turn-on knowing I have about the same amount of hair as they do. I dated a balding woman and the thing I noticed was she was much more willing to please me sexually vs. women with full heads of hair. Balding women to me are less selfish and that is what guys want. You can take them to the Burger King drive-thru for dinner and still get sex. You do that with a woman with a full head of hair and you can forget about sex for a month."

—Poster to the Hair Loss Forum on www.hairsite.com, in response to the question "Will you date a woman who is bald because she is rich?"

"This is just silly. We were told by your publishers that you were taking this book seriously. This is dumb."

—Keith and the Girl, hosts of a free comedy show and podcast at www.keithandthegirl.com

"A better question would be who would you rather fuck, a guy with a pussy or a chick with a dick. That's a question that deals with the division between appearance and reality, and between public and private lives. It gets to the heart of the nature of sexuality and the definition of gender. It's a far more fascinating query. But to answer your dumber question: The fellow with tits wins."

—My friend Jon, who has far too much free time to think about shit

THE FIGHT

Much like in the Battle of the Sexes between Bobby Riggs and Billie Jean King, the male competitor goes into the match wildly overconfident, especially for a little dude with boobs. The Large Balding Woman takes advantage of this hubris, giving him a left to the right tit and a right to the left nut. While he is keeled over, she yanks him by his man bra to the ground and then sits on his face, suffocating him. His lame attempts to pull her hair are in vain, as she is bald.

THE WINNER

LARGE BALDING WOMAN (KO)

BILL AND TED

ALLIES: Napoleon "a short dead dude" Bonaparte; So-crates Johnson; Miss of Arc; Dave Beeth Oven; and others

ENEMIES: Ted's a-hole father; their history teacher

TIME TRAVEL MACHINE: Phone booth

TAGLINES: "Be excellent to each other."; "Party on, dudes."

PERPLEXING QUESTION #1: How has Keanu Reeves stumbled ass-backward into so many cool movies?

PERPLEXING QUESTION #2: How'd one of these guys become a megastar and the other one could be on "Where are they now?"

PERPLEXING QUESTION #3: Might Keanu Reeves's most powerful, emotive performance have been in Paula Abdul's video for "Rush, Rush"? Hurry, hurry, think about it.

SEQUELS: 1

DANGER THEY FACE: Flunking out of high school

MARTY McFLY AND DOC

ALLIES: Each other; George McFly

ENEMIES: Libyan terrorists in search of missing plutonium; Biff Tannen

TIME TRAVEL MACHINE: DeLorean

TAGLINE: "Where we're going, we don't need roads."

EFFECT ON ELEMENTARY SCHOOL #1: Referring to my lunchbox as my "flux capacitor"

EFFECT ON ELEMENTARY SCHOOL #2: Asking bus driver to take it to 88, just to see what would happen

SEQUELS: 2

DANGER THEY FACE: Marty— flunking out of existence; Doc—being shot and killed

STAKES: Having to undo the damage done by traveling back in time

COOL TRICKS: "Inventing" the skateboard; teaching "Johnny B. Goode" to Chuck Berry

BILL AND TED

STAKES: World Peace and Ultimate Truth hinge on them passing history and becoming the Wyld Stallyns

COOL TRICK: Once they realize they can go back in time, they have already done so, thanks to the predestination paradox, wherein they exist in two temporal planes contemporaneously (which also allows them to give themselves advice they necessarily cannot follow).

OCCUPATIONS: High school seniors; aspiring rock musicians

LOVE INTERESTS: Elizabeth and Joanna, medieval princesses

COMIC BOOK: Yep

VIDEO GAME: Uh-huh

SPIN-OFF ANIMATED SERIES: Definitely

DISTURBINGLY HOT MATERNAL FIGURE: Bill's stepmom, Missy, who's only three years older than he is

MARTY McFLY AND DOC

OCCUPATIONS: Marty—high school senior and aspiring rock musician; Doc—eccentric scientist

LOVE INTEREST: Marty had Jennifer Parker in 1985 and, disturbingly, his own mother thirty years earlier

COMIC BOOK: Absolutely

VIDEO GAME: For sure

SPIN-OFF ANIMATED SERIES: Of course

DISTURBINGLY HOT MATERNAL FIGURE: Marty's mom, in 1955

EXPERT ANALYSIS

"This would probably be about the shortest and most non-aggressive smackdown in history! If these two parties were to get into enough of a confrontation to resort to fisticuffs in the first place, Bill and Ted would likely start by pointing out they're totally weak and couldn't possibly fight. They would probably then offer Marty tickets to Water Loop water slides. Failing that, Bill and Ted would create a diversion ("Oh look, it's Doc Brown in a flying train!") and take off (possibly giving Marty a melvin before making a hasty exit). Either way, Marty would probably breathe a sigh of relief (or a gasp of pain in the melvin scenario) as I don't think he's the type to want to get into a physical fight, either. So I guess my final analysis would be they'd both be winners, since they would avoid fighting in the first place!"

—Linda Kay, www.billandted.org, the #1 Bill and Ted fan site

"Now this is a tricky one. Both groups are highly experienced in the ways of time travel, but I'd have to give the advantage to Bill and Ted. Granted, these two may not seem all that bright, especially when compared to the genius of the Doc, but for what they lack in scientific smarts, they quickly make up for with creative conviction. Allow me to explain. In the *Back to the Future* films, whenever something goes wrong, Marty and Doc have to hop in the ol' DeLorean, hit 88 mph and off they go to solve their problems. Bill and Ted used to do something similar with their phone booth, but eventually they discovered that they didn't even NEED to physically go back in time. When they battled with Nomolos in *Bogus Journey*, all they had to do to defeat him was go back in time WITH THEIR MINDS to make changes in present time. Last but not least, let's not forget that these two beat the Reaper and came back from the dead. All Marty and the Doc ever beat was Biff Tannen and some disgruntled Libyans. Big whoop. Don't fear the Reaper . . . Wyld Stallyns Rule!"

—Roger Barr, www.i-mockery.com

THE FIGHT

With this battle taking place in the past, present, and future, Bill and Ted's use of Billy "Mister" the Kid and Bob Genghis Khan gives them a momentary edge, but Marty and Doc's superior intelligence and access to plutonium allow them to explode San Dimas's heroes and their historical cocombatants into smithereens, thereby forever changing the course of world history.

THE WINNER

MARTY McFLY AND DOC (KO)

JUDAS

ALLIES: Not so many anymore

ENEMIES: Christians

TACTICAL MANEUVER: Identified Jesus to arresting soldiers, like they couldn't tell who he was from the velvet paintings.

LOYALTY: Maybe not his strongest quality

UNCOOL MOVE: Getting the Son of God killed

NAME SYNONYMOUS WITH: Betrayal

WHY'D HE DO IT?: Evil Jews told him to, plus that Jesus was a show-off with his miracles.

REWARD FOR SELLING OUT: Thirty pieces of silver

GUILT: Appropriately great, although crying won't bring Christ back.

PUNISHMENT: Hanged himself or his gut burst and his bowels gushed out—either way, it wasn't good.

TRADEMARK FIGHTING MOVE: The Kiss of Death

ATTIRE: Sandals, robe

BENEDICT ARNOLD

ALLIES: First Americans, then British

ENEMIES: First British, then Americans

TACTICAL MANEUVER: Betray own troops, surrender the fort

LOYALTY: To the highest bidder

UNCOOL MOVE: Selling out his troops and switching sides in the middle of a war

NAME SYNONYMOUS WITH: Treason

WHY'D HE DO IT?: Was passed over for a promotion; not given credit for his military accomplishments; in debt

REWARD FOR SELLING OUT: Was supposed to be twenty grand; became six when the large plot failed.

GUILT: None

PUNISHMENT: None

TRADEMARK FIGHTING MOVE: The "Trick 'em and Dick 'em, Use 'em and Abuse 'em" combo

ATTIRE: Funny pointy hat

JUDAS

PERPLEXING QUESTION #1: Why did Jesus allow Judas to betray him?

PERPLEXING QUESTION #2: If Jesus foresaw his betrayal, does that not mean Judas had no free will, and hence no moral culpability?

PERPLEXING QUESTION #3: If sacrificing Jesus was necessary to save humanity, why was Judas punished with eternal hellfire?

EXCUSE #1: It wasn't him, it was the media.

EXCUSE #2: Well, the dude did die for *your* sins.

BENEDICT ARNOLD

PERPLEXING QUESTION #1: How did they fight in the pointy hats and funny costumes?

PERPLEXING QUESTION #2: Why was he named after a brunch dish?

PERPLEXING QUESTION #3: Did he at least do a hot slave girl, like Jefferson did?

EXCUSE #1: Betray and Surrender is actually an extremely advanced military move.

EXCUSE #2: Revolution Schmevolution—a brother's got to get paid.

EXPERT ANALYSIS

"I don't know anything about Judas Iscariot but I do know a lot about Benedict Arnold. He was a small but muscular man with penetrating eyes and a beak-like nose. He was also fearless and one of America's best combat officers until he turned traitor. General Arnold was also an expert marksman with a pistol and challenged a number of men to pistol duels during his lifetime. His truculent personality made him many enemies but he was also beloved and respected by his fellow fighting officers, including George Washington. Arnold was also a gentleman and, in accordance with the accepted code of conduct at the time, he would have fought a duel with pistols with an antagonist. Arnold was a dangerous opponent who would have coolly taken aim with his flintlock and shot to kill."

—Arthur S. Lefkowitz, author,
Benedict Arnold's Army

"Arnold would appear to be a safe bet. He was, after all, a soldier, a professional fighter. Judas was a . . . well, we don't really know what Judas was. Which is too bad, because it could make a difference. If he was a fisherman, like Peter, he might have been a pretty tough hombre, hauling all those nets all day. If he was a tax guy, like Paul (Paul was a tax guy, wasn't he?), then Judas was probably a pretty wimpy guy, an A.D. 31 version of a guy who works at the Department of Motor Vehicles. In any event, we know Arnold was short, burly, and damned tough. He was shot twice, had his leg crushed by a horse, and married a woman half his age and lived to tell about it all. As for Judas, one little setback and he runs off and hangs himself. That shows a serious weakness of character. As a professional historian, my thirty pieces of silver are on Benedict Arnold."

—Jim Nelson, author,
Benedict Arnold's Navy

THE FIGHT

Unlike most fighters who credit Jesus for helping them defeat their opponents, Judas actually has Christ fighting with him against Benedict Arnold and his Revolutionary Army. He quickly negates this advantage, however, by offering the Lord to Arnold in exchange for fifty bucks and a Yankee pot roast. Arnold then surrenders his army for three pairs of sandals and a white robe. In the end, a betrayed army is no match for a betrayed Savior, as Father, Son, and Holy Ghost team up to deliver a Day of Judgment.

THE WINNER

BENEDICT ARNOLD (GOD ON HIS SIDE)

CONFLICT FOR THE CONFEDERACY
DAVID DUKE
vs.
DAISY DUKE

DAVID DUKE

ALLIES: Knights in White Satin

ENEMIES: None: everybody loves the Klan and its message of peace and tolerance.

GOAL: Bring the oppressed white race back to a position of power.

TRADEMARK FIGHTING MOVE: The Burning Right Cross

COMMON MISCONCEPTION: According to him, he's not a racist—he's a "racial realist."

UNSUCCESSFUL ATTEMPTS: To run for senator, governor, president

BEST-KNOWN GIG: Grand Wizard of the KKK

FAVORITE OFFENSIVE SYMBOL: Swastika

THE NEXT LIFE: He will come back as a black Jewish gay woman

SCARY FACT: Received 60 percent of the white vote in the primary of the 1990 Louisiana Senate race; made it to a runoff for governor in 1991.

DAISY DUKE

ALLIES: Bo and Luke Duke; Uncle Jessie

ENEMIES: Boss Hogg; Roscoe P. Coltrane

GOAL: Keep everything very well trimmed so the eponymous cut-off jean shorts don't show too much.

TRADEMARK FIGHTING MOVE: Flirt with three dudes, watch them beat each other to death over her.

COMMON MISCONCEPTION: The tissues next to my Catherine Bach Daisy Duke poster are because I have a cold.

UNSUCCESSFUL ATTEMPTS: To find a man, which was probably the least realistic thing about that whole ridiculous show

BEST-KNOWN GIG: Waitress at the Boss Hogg–owned Boar's Nest

FAVORITE OFFENSIVE SYMBOL: Confederate flag

THE NEXT LIFE: She returned in 2005 as a blonde who couldn't even hold her own with two guys who couldn't act.

DAVID DUKE

LITTLE-KNOWN FACT: Under the pseudonym Dorothy Vanderbilt, in 1976 Duke published a self-help book for women called *Finders Keepers* that gave advice to women on fellatio, analingus, and anal sex. Really.

9/11: Blames the Jews, which, as conspiracy theories go, is a pretty tricky one to work out in your head.

INTEGRATION: Considers it racial genocide, which is kind of insulting to real genocides.

DAISY DUKE

SCARY FACT: Catherine Bach is all AARP now, which makes things a little confusing and weird.

LITTLE-KNOWN FACT: Daisy Duke owns a copy of *Finders Keepers* and is now the world's premier analingus expert.

9/11: Also blames the Jews.

INTEGRATION: Well, how many brothers did you see on that show?

THE FIGHT

Buoyed by a plethora of anonymous e-mail support, David Duke brings the whole force of the mighty, proud White Supremacist movement to his battle, which turns out to be six Jeff Foxworthy look-alikes who immediately defect to Daisy Duke's side when she puts her index finger in her mouth and winks. The scorned Grand Wizard is driven in his Klan robes into Compton, where he is dropped off at a Nation of Islam meeting.

THE WINNER

DAISY DUKE (KO)

PHILOSOPHER/CARTOON DOG BATTLE

PLATO
VS.
PLUTO

PLATO

MAJOR ACCOMPLISHMENTS: He laid the foundation for Western philosophy and established the Academy in Athens, the first institution of higher learning in the Western world.

ALLIES: Reason; logic; young and attractive boys who weren't quite ready for the depths of his rhetoric

ENEMIES: Ignorance; the parents of those young and attractive boys

TEACHER: Socrates, who also wasn't the straightest of arrows

STUDENTS: Aristotle; other young and curious men who were interested in a little late-night philosophy

FORMATIVE EXPERIENCE: The trial of Socrates

DIALOGUES: Used to teach philosophy, logic, rhetoric.

GREAT WORK: *The Republic*

IDEAL LEADER: The Philosopher King

PLUTO

MAJOR ACCOMPLISHMENT: Managed to be the nontalking dog of a talking mouse.

ALLIES: Fifi the Pike; Ronnie the St. Bernard puppy

ENEMIES: Chip 'n' Dale; Butch the Bulldog; stupid anthropomorphic Goofy

TEACHER: Mickey Mouse

STUDENTS: We can all learn from his boundless energy and joie de vivre.

FORMATIVE EXPERIENCE: Unrequited love for Dinah the Dachshund

DIALOGUES: None, as he doesn't talk, unlike that bastard Goofy

GREAT WORK: *Bone Trouble*

IDEAL LEADER: The Philosopher King

THEORY OF FORMS: Round is funny, square not so much.

QUESTION RAISED BY HIS WORK: How come Goofy, who is also a goddamned dog, gets to talk and wear pants and he doesn't?

RECURRING THEME IN HIS WORK: Dog-mouse loyalty

PLATO

THEORY OF FORMS: The human experience is a shadow of a higher realm, in which exist the forms, or the truth behind the shadows—perfect, unchanging ideals we use to decipher the empirical world.

QUESTION RAISED BY HIS WORK: Should the Unity of Forms, or Ultimate Form, be equated with the concept of God?

RECURRING THEME IN HIS WORK: Man-boy love, which isn't something one necessarily feels comfortable discussing in Philosophy 101.

TRADEMARK FIGHTING MOVE: The Cupping Hand of Logic

WACKY BLOOPER: When in describing political systems to Apollodorus and Antiphon, he said "timocracy" when he meant "oligarchy." They were all ROTFL!

PLUTO

TRADEMARK FIGHTING MOVE: The Lick of Death

WACKY BLOOPER: When, in *Playful Pluto,* he got stuck in a piece of flypaper and could not get out.

EXPERT ANALYSIS

"One story has it that the author of *The Republic* was given the name 'Plato,' meaning 'broad,' by his wrestling coach, as he was very buff, and there is nothing gay at all about your ancient Greek wrestling coach giving you a very buff name. Pluto was named by Disney animators after the dwarf planet Pluto, which in turn was named after the god of the underworld. While the god of the underworld may sound intimidating, Pluto is a cartoon dog. Unlike Goofy, Pluto cannot walk upright or speak. He's just a dog. I predict that Pluto would prove egregiously poor at strategy (and wrestling); biting would be his only real means of attack. Even if Pluto got a good bite into Plato, Plato could just run back into his cave, which represents ignorance and a reliance on the material world, but still, it's a cave. Winner: Plato."

—Jennifer Dzuria, stand-up comedienne and blogger (www.jenisfamous.com)

"Plato. I mean, I hate to say it, but Plato's a guy and Pluto's a lovable, brain-damaged dog. The image of one of the founding fathers of modern thought stabbing or clubbing a big orange dog to death is not a pleasant one. Yeesh. Close your eyes and think about that for a while."

—Ari Voukydis, *VH1: All Access*
commentator and one-half of
the comedy team found at
www.markandari.com

"Plato would never fight Pluto. Instead, they would become instant friends. In *The Republic,* Plato says that the auxiliaries to the Philosopher King are like faithful dogs—loyal and truthful to their master. So their duel will turn into a friendship."

—T. K. Seung, philosophy professor
at the University of Texas at Austin,
author of *Plato Rediscovered*
and, most recently, *Kant: A Guide
for the Perplexed*

THE FIGHT

Out on a long walk, Pluto wanders into Plato's cave, where he strokes young minds until they ejaculate wisdom, and inserts his girthy brilliance into their once tight and undistended worldviews. The philosopher immediately takes to the cartoon dog and instructs him on the Forms and the means to creating a just and erudite society. Pluto begins to walk upright and talk, and enrolls in Plato's Academy, where, at his graduation ceremony, he uses his newfound powers of rhetoric to convince Mickey Mouse and Goofy to kill each other, then takes over the Disney empire.

THE WINNER

BOTH (LEARNING IS WINNING!)

BATTLE OF THE LITTLE PEOPLE

HOBBITS
VS.
THE SEVEN DWARFS
VS.
SMURFS

HOBBITS

TASK: Destroy the ring and save Middle Earth.

ALLY: Sir Wizard McGay

ENEMIES: Sauron; Orcs; Ringwraiths; parents of socially maladjusted *LOTR* freaks

POLITICAL SYSTEM: Agrarian democracy

OCCUPATIONS: Mostly farmers

SOCIETY: Nature-loving; peaceful; hairy

WELL-KNOWN HOBBITS: Bilbo Baggins; that funny-looking big-eyed kid from *Flipper;* former U.S. Secretary of Labor Robert Reich

SMURFS

TASK: Smurf it up and smurf it out.

OCCUPATIONS: Whatever it takes for the greater good of Smurfdom

POLITICAL SYSTEM: Communist Smurftopia

ALIASES: Leon Trotsky (Brainy Smurf); Karl Marx (Papa Smurf)

CHARACTERISTICS: They are blue, shirtless, and have tails, just like Comrade Lenin.

SOCIETY: Contains countless selfless workers and a single woman, Smurfette, whose Smurfulescent Smurfholes are available for all Smurfish desires.

SUPERPOWERS AND ABILITIES: Able to share a single woman among a large society without resorting to homicide. Also, is being adorable a superpower? Yes, you are!

IDOL: The humble, hardworking proletariat has no time for false idols.

THE SEVEN DWARFS

TASK: Protect the fairest one of all.

ALIASES: Doc; Grumpy; Dopey; Jewy; Itchy; Drippy; Tumescent

CHARACTERISTICS: Long white beards except for Dopey; condomlike hats

ALLIES: Snow White; generations of children all over the world; anyone who's ever cared for a woman only to have her leave for some taller, better-looking dude

ENEMIES: The Queen Witch

OCCUPATIONS: Whistling workers in a jewel mine

WHAT DO YOU CALL THEIR PROSTITUTES?: Heigh-Hos

SMURFS

ALLIES: They need none, as they band together as one for the greater good. But anyone who loves Smurfy cuteness!

ENEMIES: Gargamel the ugly capitalist, who wishes to turn them into gold; his cat Azrael, who is so not cute

SECRET AGENDA: Make kids listen to Communist classical music.

DIET: They eat Smurfberries, which sounds like a vulgar euphemism but is not.

EXPERT ANALYSIS

"Well, if this fight were to actually take place—and it were to take place with Frodo/Sam/Merry/Pippin after they'd survived *The Lord of the Rings*—they'd beat the shit out of the other two groups. However, if the Seven Dwarfs from Snow White's land were also a part of the *Lord of the Rings* universe, they would have full combat training, mithril armor and weaponry...and a thirst for blood. Having said that— Dopey with an axe could very well kill everyone else in a battle of JarJarian proportions!"

—Harry Knowles, film critic for *Penthouse,* founder of the renowned film site www.aintitcool.com

"The obvious first choice would be the Hobbits. They can fight, they wear armor sometimes, and their bare feet give them extra mobility. The Seven Dwarfs are like some weird kind of dwarf commune, where they name each other after emotions, and do not carry battle-axes. As for Smurfs, they are only three apples high, so in an all-out brawl with a Hobbit in, say, a boxing ring, the Hobbit would probably win. However, Smurfs never act alone. Any fight for them would be a war involving the whole village. Their village is hidden, which is a huge asset in any war. And the Smurfs have Papa Smurf, who is friends with Father Time and Mother Earth, both powerful allies. I think the Smurfs would win this fight. They are hardworking, have a strong team spirit, have access to magical powers, and have a hidden village."

—J. Marc Schmidt, graphic novelist and author of the Web essay "Socio-Political Themes in the Smurfs," which can be seen at http://jmarcs.web.fc2.com/

"The Smurfs' guiding principle is agenda-driven loyalty. This paralyzes them with inflexibility and easily targeted blind spots. The Seven Dwarfs are self-aware and dangerously imbalanced. It's no wonder their weapon of choice is a pickaxe. They should consider who they are at their deepest rather than being so manipulated by someone else's vision of life, which blocks their chi and weakens them. They will defeat themselves. Conversely, the Hobbits are elemental, rooted, focused, and connected to the big picture. They will have no problem going with the flow. Clearly this is a battle of the centered vs. the un-centered. The Hobbits will win."

—Joseph Cardillo, author of *Bow to Life: 365 Secrets from the Martial Arts for Daily Life* and *Be Like Water: Practical Wisdom from the Martial Arts*

THE FIGHT

The Dwarfs have pickaxes and the Smurfs have the strength of their Marxist principles, but the Hobbits throw money at the problem, burying their adversaries under piles of cash from *LOTR* ticket sales and merchandising.

THE WINNER

HOBBITS (KO)

MAD COW

PROBLEM: Fatal neurodegenerative disease

SCIENTIFIC NAME: Bovine spongiform encephalopathy

CRAP DEAL: In the United Kingdom, 179,000 cattle were infected and 4.4 million cows were killed as a precautionary measure.

ALLIES: Syphilitic sheep; herpes hamster

ENEMIES: Freaked-out Brits who started a cowicide

HOW SHE GOT IT: By humans feeding herbivores ground-up parts of other cows, which leads one to believe it should be called "mad people disease."

TRADEMARK FIGHTING MOVE: The Quarter Pounder with Death

SCIENTIFIC VIEW ON THE DISEASE'S ORIGIN: Infectious prion proteins developed through spontaneous moo-tation

SAD COW

PROBLEMS: Extremely moo-dy (yes, yes, moo jokes!); fraught with udder malaise

SCIENTIFIC NAME: Bovine gloomiform melancholopathy

CRAP DEAL: No one wants to milk her, ask her how she's feeling.

ALLIES: Pessimistic Bunny; Grumpy Bear

ENEMIES: Optimistic Orangutan; Perky Parrot

HOW SHE GOT IT: Parents too busy vapidly chewing cud to give her the attention and love she craved and needed.

TRADEMARK FIGHTING MOVE: Why does it matter? No one will notice anyway.

SCIENTIFIC VIEW ON THE DISEASE'S ORIGIN: Started with the chewing of chronically depressed grass.

THE FIGHT

Sad Cow just wants to be left alone to listen to the Smiths and write free-form confessional poetry. Mad Cow is understandably pissed off about rotting from the inside and bleeding from the eyes, and charges at Sad Cow just as she has begun her daily call to the suicide hotline, where they always hear her moos as cries for help. Mad Cow murders Sad Cow and infects her dead carcass, making her outside look like her inside felt. Farmers grind up Sad Cow and feed her to cattle, creating a new breed of diseased and depressed bovine that might kill itself before it kills you.

THE WINNER

MAD COW (KO)

BEAT-OFF OF THE DYNAMIC DIDDLERS
PEE-WEE HERMAN
vs.
GEORGE MICHAEL

PEE-WEE HERMAN

ALLIES: Fellow masturbators, who feel the punishment didn't fit the crime. Although a punishment that did fit the crime would be a kinky-ass punishment.

ENEMIES: Shocked and horrified parents forced to actually discuss sex with their children

MUG SHOT: He had long hair and a goatee, which everyone found shocking too, like he's supposed to go into a porn theater dressed as Pee-wee Herman.

HIS EFFECT ON MY HIGH SCHOOL EXPERIENCE: An endless onslaught of lame Pee-wee Herman jokes, to which you will now be subjected

LAME PEE-WEE HERMAN JOKE #1: Did you hear Pee-wee declined representation? He figures he can get himself off!

LAME PEE-WEE HERMAN JOKE #2: Did you hear about the new Pee-wee Herman doll? It pulls its own string!

LAME PEE-WEE HERMAN JOKE #3: What did Jeffrey Dahmer say to Pee-wee Herman? Don't play with your food!

GEORGE MICHAEL

ALLIES: Andrew Ridgeley; Elton John

ENEMY: The undercover cop at a public toilet in a park in Beverly Hills

HIS EFFECT ON MY JUNIOR HIGH SCHOOL EXPERIENCE: Awkwardly slow-dancing to "Father Figure," "One More Try," and "Careless Whisper" at bar and bat mitzvahs

WHY HE'S NEVER GOING TO DANCE AGAIN: Guilty feet have got no rhythm.

WHY HE WANTS YOUR SEX: Because sex is natural and sex is fun, and sex is best when it's one-on-one.

HIS GREATEST SUCCESS: *Faith*, which has sold over 20 million records to date

REAL NAME: Georgios-Kyriacos Panayiotou (Why'd he change it?)

TIP-OFFS TO HIS SEXUAL ORIENTATION: The pastel short shorts, frosted hair, and smiley bouncy disposition in the "Wake Me Up Before You Go-Go" video

PEE-WEE HERMAN

HIS GREATEST SUCCESS: *Pee-wee's Big Adventure,* which cost only $6 million to make and took in $45 million at the box office

REAL NAME: Paul Reubens (born Paul Rubenfeld)

COSTARS: Phil Hartman; Laurence Fishburne; Jambi the Genie; a talking chair on *Pee-wee's Playhouse*

QUESTION: If you love porn so much, why don't you marry it?

THE SECRET WORD: Pervert. AAAAAHHHHHH!!!

GEORGE MICHAEL

TESTAMENT TO HIS GENEROSITY: Though he is gay, he granted heterosexual teenage boys the stupidly hot Cindy Crawford in a bathtub *Freedom '90* video.

NOT SO FUN GAME HE PLAYED: I'll show you mine, you'll show me yours, I'll arrest you for engaging in a lewd act.

THE FIGHT

Neither man has any interest in fighting, as they are too busy beating themselves.

THE WINNER

NONE (DOUBLE DQ DUE TO MASTURBATIONAL PREOCCUPATION)

CAP'N CRUNCH

GIVEN NAME: Horatio Magellan Crunch. Really.

FIRST APPEARANCE: 1963

LITTLE-KNOWN FACT: Crunchberries immediately stimulate puberty in children.

DISTINGUISHING FEATURES: Funny sailor outfit; overbearing enthusiasm

ALLIES: The Trix Rabbit; Cocoa Puffs Cuckoo

ENEMIES: "Barefoot Pirate" Jean LaFoote and the evil Soggies, who attempt to sog out his cereal's crunchiness

NUTRITIONAL VALUE: Just below Pop Rocks, above SweeTarts

EXTREMELY COOL PRIZE IN BOX: A toy whistle in Cap'n Crunch boxes in the early '70s emitted a tone at 2600 hertz, which was found to be the perfect tone to disconnect one end of a phone call and get the still-connected side into operator mode. The whistle inspired the creation of blue boxes, which could reproduce other tones used by the phone company. No lie.

TONY THE TIGER

GIVEN NAME: Antonius Tigris (He is Greek, although he denies it.)

FIRST APPEARANCE: 1952

COMPETITION: Tony wasn't always the lone face of Frosted Flakes, sharing mascot status in the '50s with Katy the Kangaroo, Elmo the Elephant, and Newt the Gnu. Tony ate them. They were grrreat. (Kellogg's official version is that Katy, Elmo, and Newt were phased out. Don't believe them.)

LITTLE-KNOWN FACT: If frosted properly, the flakes are aphrodisiacs.

DISTINGUISHING FEATURES: Unnecessary scarf; overbearing enthusiasm

ALLIES: His creatively named daughter Antoinette, son Tony Jr., and wife Mrs. Tony

ENEMIES: Big-game cereal hunters

DARK SECRET: If you eat another cereal in his presence, he will fucking kill you.

NUTRITIONAL VALUE: Well, the flakes would be healthy if they weren't covered in cocaine.

CAP'N CRUNCH

BACKGROUND: Growing up, Horatio Crunch never wanted to be a pirate, aspiring instead for a career in musical theater. But back in those days these were not things cartoons could discuss, and his parents quickly bought him a cutlass and sailor suit, telling him to never speak of this dream again. He stores his *My Fair Lady* record in the hull of the Good Ship Guppy and still listens to it wistfully, when he is not fighting off the Soggies.

TONY THE TIGER

HORRIFIC PRIZE IN BOX: The fingers and toes of misbehaving toddlers

BACKGROUND: Moving as a youth from his native Newark, New Jersey, to the Sumatran jungle, a young and enterprising Tony searched far and wide for a tasty breakfast alternative to deer, antelope, and abandoned tiger cubs. At first, he leaned toward honey-coated rhinoceros, but the difficulty in successfully killing a rhinoceros and coating it in honey made this unfeasible. He thought of Leopard Loops, but leopard does not loop easily, and the public was not ready for furry cereal. Finally, he came upon the recipe for Frosted Flakes, and a phenomenon was born. But he still always puts a little leopard and rhino in his bowls of the cereal.

EXPERT ANALYSIS

"Cap'n Crunch vs. Tony the Tiger — it's an old fighting man against a pussycat. What do you think?"

—Don Markstein, www.toonopedia. com, the world's first hypertext encyclopedia of toons

"Wow! Cap'n vs. Tony? These two both fight on the side of good. Whatever turned one against the other would nonetheless result in a lot of spilled milk. I'd give the nod to Tony for his stealth (assuming he can keep his mouth shut until after the attack), but the Cap'n would certainly leave a couple of holes in Tony's rug."

—Topher Ellis, Topher's Breakfast Cereal Character Guide (www. lavasurfer.com/cereal-guide.html)

"An elderly sailor with phony epaulets versus a lip-smacking tiger? Not the toughest call to make. Even with his disturbing team of underage shipmates to back him up, I don't think the Cap'n has it in him to best the duke of beasts. He might be able to grab a rapier and hold Tony off long enough to scurry up the mizzen-mast, and his sea legs might give him an advantage if the battle takes place on deck. But his delusions of admiralty, not to mention overconfidence spawned by past victories over the Soggies, are bound to send him back into the breach until he is devoured by the anthropomorphic tiger."

—Dale Dobson, humorist for *Cracked, National Lampoon,* and *Yankee Pot Roast,* who has eaten many bowls of Cap'n Crunch in his lifetime, but has traditionally eschewed Tony's cornflakes-plus-sugar recipe for reasons that, upon present reflection, are neither sensible nor consistent

THE FIGHT

Cap'n Crunch sails his ship through the wall of the Hollywood studio where Tony is filming a Frosted Flakes commercial, creating an immediate You Tube sensation when Tony shouts "They're Grrrr-FUCK!" and, incensed, begins to eat the Cap'n's crew whole. The Cap'n attempts to "crunch-a-tize" the man-eating beast, but he is quickly chomped into nothing more than a sailor cap and a mustache.

THE WINNER

TONY THE TIGER (KO)

CEREAL BATTLE #2
BOO BERRY
vs.
FRANKEN BERRY

BOO BERRY

CIVILIAN IDENTITY: Boutros-Boutros Berry

FIRST APPEARANCE: 1973

SUPERPOWERS AND ABILITIES: Turns milk blue; creeps kids out

DISTINGUISHING FEATURES: Droopy junkie eyes; voice like Peter Lorre; inexplicable top hat and bow tie

ENEMIES: Franken Berry; Count Chocula; Yummy Mummy*

ALLIES: The nice lady at the methadone clinic; Fruit Brute*

NUTRITIONAL VALUE: Provides nine vitamins and minerals, which is also true of tube socks. Contains 4,000 percent of the daily recommended allowance of blue marshmallows.

LAME PRIZE IN BOX: "Wacky Sticky Thing"

FRANKEN BERRY

CIVILIAN IDENTITY: Shmuel Berryberg

FIRST APPEARANCE: 1971

SUPERPOWERS AND ABILITIES: Turns milk pink; morphs into prepubescent boy on the Internet

DISTINGUISHING FEATURES: Phallic head bolt on right temple; antennae on cheeks; pedophil-ish leer

ENEMIES: Boo Berry; Count Chocula; Fruit Brute; the congressmen and -women responsible for Megan's Law

ALLIES: Children "all over the world"; Yummy Mummy; anyone who understands the special needs of those hopelessly devoted to man/boy love

NUTRITIONAL VALUE: Provides nine vitamins and minerals, which is "a good reason to give me what I need."

LAME PROMOTION: Franken Berry Pez dispenser, which provided children the only food less healthy than Franken Berry cereal

*incarcerated

BOO BERRY

BACKGROUND: Two years after the first characters in General Mills's ill-conceived Monster-themed line, Count Chocula and Franken Berry, were introduced in 1971, blueberry-flavored Boo Berry made its first appearance, due to inaccurate studies that claimed an important part of any child's diet are nightmares. His best friend, Fruit Brute, showed up a year later, only to be discontinued in 1983 due to negligible sales. This devastating event led to the Brute's attempted murder of the wildly popular Count Chocula, and further intensified Boo's already crippling heroin addiction. An embarrassing makeover in the late '90s did not help. The unspoken shame of the General Mills family, Boo's distribution is extremely low and sporadic, despite a hard-core, cultlike fan base (see www.i_mockery. com/booberry/fans.htm), which is forced to hoard the cereal during its period of increased availability around Halloween.

FRANKEN BERRY

BACKGROUND: Strawberry-flavored Franken Berry was first introduced by General Mills in 1971 along with Count Chocula, as part of General Mills's drug-induced monster cereal concept. Unable to appear with children in commercials due to "oppressive" legislation that "hates me because I love," Franken Berry found an ally when child pornographer Yummy Mummy was introduced by General Mills in 1988, only to be discontinued in 1993 due to lagging sales and a few incriminating images. In an attempt to boost his own poor sales, Franken Berry was given a makeover that makes him look like a piece of toast on Ecstasy. Often mentioned by Conan O'Brien as his favorite cereal because it turns the milk pink, and a recurring character on the TV show *Family Guy*, Franken Berry still has difficulty being stocked in supermarkets except in late October, leaving him lots of time for chat rooms.

EXPERT ANALYSIS

"Boo Berry would win, there's simply no doubt about it. He means business and his cereal is tastier than Franken Berry and Count Chocula combined. Being a spirit, he could possess Franken Berry and make that big clumsy pink bastard walk off a cliff into a boiling pit of his own rancid strawberry cereal."

—Roger Barr, host of "The Unofficial Boo Berry Page" (www.i-mockery.com/booberry/), whose Boo Berry expertise has been featured on VH1's *Totally Obsessed,* The Food Network's *Unwrapped,* and Comedy Central's *The Daily Show*

"Boo Berry would easily win that one. Franken Berry is a wuss. He's afraid of his own shadow. Boo Berry is afraid of no one."

—Topher Ellis, Topher's Breakfast Cereal Character Guide (www.lavasurfer.com/cereal-guide.html)

"While Franken Berry is bound to the material world, Boo Berry has the advantage of an astro body. Fighting him is like trying to punch at a vibration. The astro plane is filled with angels, monsters, demons, and artists of all kinds. One person's chi in the astro world is more powerful than a nuclear reactor. Franken Berry can't differentiate between what he wants and what he needs. He needs a course in consciousness studies. He can't win."

—Joseph Cardillo, author of *Bow to Life: 365 Secrets from the Martial Arts for Daily Life* and *Be Like Water: Practical Wisdom from the Martial Arts*

"Franken Berry would probably win out over Boo Berry, but that's only because of his superior bulk and the fact that it's hard for an immaterial guy to land a punch."

—Don Markstein, of Don Markstein's Toonopedia Guide to Cartoon Characters (www.toonopedia.com)

THE FIGHT

As both Berries wait outside General Mills corporate headquarters to plead for increased distribution, an argument ensues over whose cereal is more deserving. Franken threatens Boo, to which B.B. responds, "What are you going to do, kill me? I'm a ghost!" He proceeds to stuff Franken's head in a box of Boo Berry cereal, suffocating him.

THE WINNER

BOO BERRY (KO)

IT ALL CHANGES AFTER PUBERTY FEUD
TICKLE ME ELMO
vs.
FUCK ME DOLL

TICKLE ME ELMO

ALLY: Big Bird

ENEMIES: Parents who didn't get their screaming children the stupid toy in the mid-1990s and now face deeply resentful adolescents

BASED ON: An extremely adorable and uncomplicated *Sesame Street* character who talks like a baby and is infinitely less interesting than old-school *Sesame Street*ers like manic Grover, filthy Oscar the Grouch, gay Bert and Ernie, or imaginary Mister Snuffleupagus.

COST: Due to short supply, the thirty-dollar doll was being sold for as much as $1,500 in 1996.

UNFORTUNATE CIRCUMSTANCE: A clerk at Wal-Mart was trampled on December 14, 1996, when adults saw him with one of the few remaining Elmos and bum-rushed him; he suffered a pulled hamstring, broken rib, and concussion.

FEATURES: When squeezed, Elmo chortles; when squeezed three times in a row, he shakes and laughs uncontrollably. If squeezed a hundred times in a row, he calls you a pervert and reports you to the authorities.

FUCK ME DOLL

ALLY: Pervy Pervenberg

ENEMY: Pervy Pervenberg's frigid, overtired, poorly lubricated wife

BASED ON: Attractive nonsynthetic women

COST: Cheap vinyl ones are just $50, midrange latex ones are between $100 and $200, and the expensive silicone ones can cost over a grand.

HOW I KNOW THAT: Steadfast journalistic research; why?

DANGERS: Health risk from vinyl chloride; allergies to latex; getting caught midcoitus by a college roommate who really should *not* have left his job at the student library early that day, whether or not the head librarian said it was okay.

FEATURES: The more expensive dolls have flexible joints for a variety of positions.

OPTIONAL FEATURES: Pelvic thruster motor, audio capability

TICKLE ME ELMO

FOLLOW-UP TICKLE ME TOYS: Tickle Me Ernie; Tickle Me Big Bird; Tickle Me Cookie Monster— none of which did nearly as well, as they rang false.

THE NEW TICKLE ME ELMO: Rolls around on the floor hitting the ground and begging the tickler to stop.

TRADEMARK FIGHTING MOVE: The Desperate Mother Heartclench

FUCK ME DOLL

ALTERNATIVES: Paying a real woman with a mechanical vagina; sticking one's penis into chocolate and tapioca puddings; a lifetime of intense psychotherapy

TRADEMARK FIGHTING MOVE: Trapping you in her shame holes

THE FIGHT

Tickle Me Elmo is intrigued by his playmate and soon realizes giggly squeezetime has been replaced by something far more squishy and funny-feeling. Elmo enters the soft secret hideaway, and he feels very ticklish in there. Then a week later he feels itchyish, drippyish, and burnyish, and has to visit the Sesame Street Health Clinic for a few tests.

THE WINNER

FUCK ME DOLL (TKO, GONORRHEA)

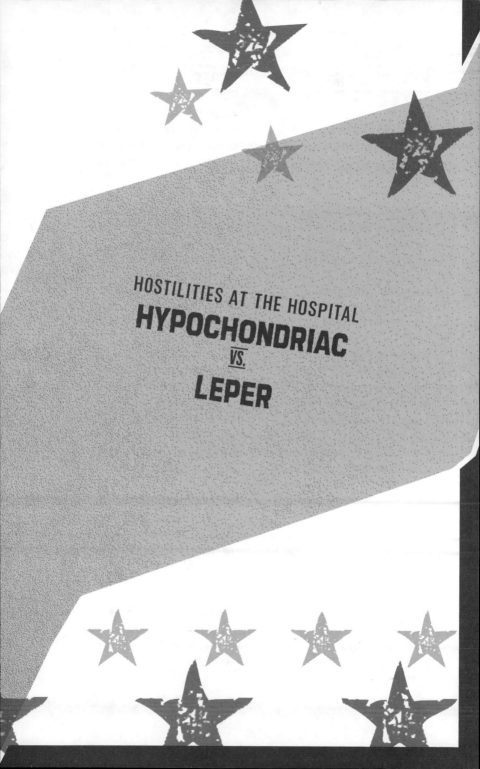

HOSTILITIES AT THE HOSPITAL
HYPOCHONDRIAC
VS.
LEPER

HYPOCHONDRIAC

AILMENT #1: Believes he just caught cancer from a dirty park bench, and he just felt it spread from his left leg to his right leg.

AILMENT #2: That undercooked piece of chicken from two years ago finally caught up with him, potentially fatally.

AILMENT #3: Latent brain aneurysm, which has no signs and will kill him instantly

DIAGNOSIS #1: Your heart's not "palpitating," it's "beating."

DIAGNOSIS #2: That lump on your testicle *is* your testicle.

DIAGNOSIS #3: That's not stomach cancer; you ate hot wings.

ALLIES: Other hypochondriacs, who understand and sympathize

ENEMIES: People with real medical problems, who have to listen to this shit

HOBBY: Self-diagnosing so much he'll have to start charging himself

LEPER

AILMENT: Horrific skin lesions; his nerves attacked by his own immune cells in a "Defender"-like battle over his rotting flesh

RESIDENCE: Gets to hang out with his buddies in their very own colony!

FIGHTING ADVANTAGE: Just coming near him is majorly gross.

FIGHTING DISADVANTAGE: It's hard to concentrate when your nose is falling off.

ANIMALS WITH LEPROSY: Armadillos; mangabey monkeys

HOW YOU CONTRACT LEPROSY: From having sex with armadillos and mangabey monkeys, which, weirdly enough, is so worth it.

TREATMENT: Multidrug therapy; quarantine; a whole bunch of prayer to a God who, if you think about it, could be considered responsible for your hand rotting off your wrist.

WHERE LEPROSY IS MOST COMMON: India, but only because it's the primary ingredient in Chicken Vindaloo.

HYPOCHONDRIAC

FIGHTING ADVANTAGE: Nothing to lose, as he is already convinced he's dying.

FIGHTING DISADVANTAGE: A punch to his face will give him Face AIDS.

LEPER

FIGHTING ADVANTAGE: You're never ready for someone throwing his eyeball at you.

FIGHTING DISADVANTAGE: Sticking and moving only works if one's arms and legs stay stuck to one's body.

THE FIGHT

In a show of good sportsmanship, the Leper shakes the Hypochondriac's hand prior to their bout. The Hypochondriac keels over in a psychosomatic coma.

THE WINNER

LEPER (KO)

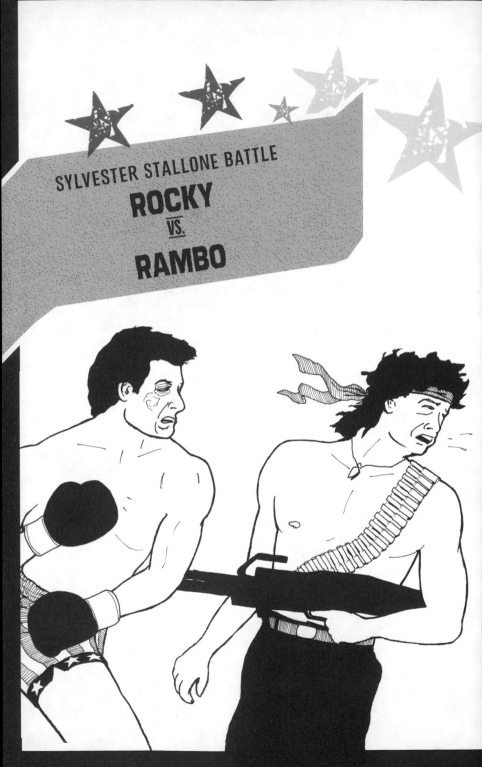

SYLVESTER STALLONE BATTLE

ROCKY
VS.
RAMBO

ROCKY

CHARACTERISTICS: Eye of the tiger; heart of a champion; illegal human growth hormone prescriptions of an actual athlete

ALLIES: Mickey; Paulie

ENEMIES: Clubber Lang; Ivan Drago

LOVE INTEREST: Adrian

DUBIOUS DECISIONS: Apollo Creed over Rocky in the first fight; *Rocky* over *Taxi Driver* and *Network* for 1976 Best Picture

BIG BREAK: Title shot against Apollo Creed

FIGHTING STYLE: Fights with his heart, which is difficult to do as it is inside his body.

TRAINING METHODS: Running stairs; beating meat

DAY JOB: Debt collector for a loan shark

DISAPPOINTMENT: Inability to out-act Mr. T, Hulk Hogan

NICKNAME: The Italian Stallion

RAMBO

CHARACTERISTICS: Bitterness, isolation, and fury, all of which are mitigated somewhat by his sweet ability to kill a man with his bare hands

ALLIES: All died in 'Nam.

ENEMIES: Evil Sheriff Will Teasle and his sadistic head deputy, Art Gault

LOVE INTEREST: None, as horrific torture while a POW created some intimacy issues

PRONE TO: Vietnam flashback–triggered psychotic breaks, which are so not cool when you're just trying to watch the fucking football game

MILITARY HONORS: Member of an Elite Special Forces unit in Vietnam, where he received a Medal of Honor

WEAPONS: Survival knife and ginormous machine gun, which looks like a classic case of overcompensating

ROCKY

INSPIRATION: Chuck Wepner, the "Bayonne Bleeder," who lasted until the fifteenth round against Muhammad Ali

VIDEO GAMES: Many

HOMETOWN: Philly, where the immense popularity of the Rocky statue highlights the lack of important nonfictional people there

RAMBO

GREATEST ACCOMPLISHMENT: Survives a National Guard rocket launcher attack; at that point, you kind of have to hand it to him and go home.

FRUSTRATION: Unlike the battlefield, society has no code of honor—although, to be fair, it also doesn't generally have minefields.

CRITICISM: The films could be considered slightly violent.

INSPIRATION: 1972 book *First Blood* by David Morrell

VIDEO GAMES: Certainly

ADMIRED BY: Ronald Reagan, which is great, because you want the Leader of the Free World looking up to a disillusioned, unstable machine-gun-toting drifter.

EXPERT ANALYSIS

"You have to figure Rambo's going to slaughter Rocky. I mean, Rocky's got spunk and all, but Rambo's got guns. And knives. And has killed hundreds of men, whereas Rocky got his ass beat by Carl Weathers. There's no way Rocky can win ... which makes him the ultimate underdog! They said he couldn't win against Mr. T! They said he couldn't win against Dolf Lundgren! But he came back! He's the champ! Rocky wins! Adrian!"

—Ari Voukydis, commentator for
VH1: All-Access and one-half
of the comedy team found at
www.markandari.com

"While Rocky might have the resilience and ring craft, his training consisted of little more than chasing chickens and running up flights of steps. How would he cope outside the ropes with a guerrilla-warfare expert like Rambo? No contest."

—Graham Thompson, author of
American Culture in the 1980s

"Rocky Balboa vs. John Rambo. It's the battle of the ages (and no, not because they're, at this point, no longer spring chickens). Sylvester Stallone is brought in as the guest ref. There will be no judges as this is a fight to the finish. Rambo starts out fast and takes an early lead as he gives Rocky a beating that would kill most men ...

BUT ... Rocky ... never quits. In the later rounds Rocky makes a comeback and looks to have Rambo beat. After twelve grueling rounds with both men bloody and bruised, Sylvester Stallone, in a SLY (groan) move, calls the fight a draw."

—Craig Zablo, webmaster, www.
stallonezone.com, the #1 Sylvester
Stallone fan site

"As much as I'd love to cheer on our favorite boxing underdog, I have a hard time believing that Rocky could beat Rambo. We're in the new millennium now and both franchises are coming to an end with one final movie each. Rocky already had his chance to shine in 'Rocky Balboa,' and while he made an impressive comeback to go toe-to-toe with the current champion, Mason 'the Line' Dixon [*Author's note:* spoiler alert], he didn't even win that fight. As of now, the final Rambo movie isn't out yet, but if you've seen the trailer, it shows John Rambo throwing one insanely ferocious punch and knocking his enemy's head clean off. Even in the prime of Rocky's career, he never came close to knocking anybody's head off like that. Rambo may be old, but anybody who can decapitate with his fists is a man you should NOT mess with under any circumstances. Sorry Rock, but I'm gonna have to throw in the towel for you on this one."

—Roger Barr, webmaster,
www.i-mockery.com

THE FIGHT

Rocky, the unknown challenger, is a huge underdog against champ Rambo, who has killed entire villages. But Balboa battles, and is winning decisively when Rambo grabs his right arm and breaks it. Rocky valiantly fights on left-handed, until Rambo breaks his left arm as well. The Italian Stallion continues to brawl with two broken arms, landing devastating combos that leave both men howling in pain. Then Rambo pulls a grenade out of his shorts and blows off both of Rocky's legs. But Rocky keeps fighting, 'cause he's got heart, at least until Rambo rips it out of his chest in the ninth round. Still, a broken-armed, legless, heartless Rocky has Rambo against the ropes and is pounding him with body shots when the Vietnam vet whips out his hunting knife and decapitates Rocky. A headless Balboa is at a distinct disadvantage, though he stays on his torso through the twelfth and final round, after which Rambo wins a controversial split decision to retain his title and Rocky's severed head yells for Adrian.

THE WINNER

RAMBO (SPLIT DECISION)

COLLISION OF THE GREAT AMERICAN GENIUSES
THOMAS EDISON
vs.
MacGYVER

THOMAS EDISON

ALLY: Fellow telegrapher and inventor Franklin Pope

ENEMY: Nikola Tesla, his former assistant and adversary in the AC/DC battle that shook us all century long (Hah! Yecccccchhhhh.)

PATENTS: 1,097 in the United States alone, although 1,081 were incremental improvements to the paper towel

EDUCATION: Had only three months of schooling, and was called "addled" by his teacher the Reverend Engle, who probably had a hard time living that one down. He was removed from that school and homeschooled by his mother.

HIS MOTHER: Invented light and sound.

LOVE INTERESTS: Married twice—both times to teenagers. Proposed to his first wife in Morse code, which is *so* slick.

RESIDENCE: Menlo Park, New Jersey, where he set up the world's first industrial research lab

MacGYVER

ALLIES: Pete Thornton; Jack Dalton; Sir Gau

ENEMIES: Murdoc, who took pictures of his victims at their moment of death and who himself almost died nearly every episode.

WHY GUN-CONTROL ADVOCATES DIG MACGYVER: He refused to carry or use a gun due to a childhood accident with a revolver that resulted in a friend's death.

EVERY SHOW: He managed to get locked in a room with something really handy.

SHOW'S CLAIM: That all the doohickeys and thingamajigs MacGyver invented on the spot were based on scientific principles, which explains why, easy as it might seem, you can't trap Stephen Hawking in a room.

TOOLS: Swiss Army knife; duct tape

WEAPONS: Chewing gum; rubber band; sock

INFLUENCE: I kept asking to be locked in rooms it turns out I really couldn't escape from.

HIS FIRST PATENT: The Electric Vote Recorder, when he was twenty-one

HIGHLIGHT: Coming up with the first device to record and reproduce sound, which was good and all, but nothing compared to when I threw a no-hitter in Little League.

MOST IMPORTANT PATENTS: The phonograph and first commercially practical incandescent lightbulb, both of which are nearly as significant as Ron Popeil's Inside-the-Shell Electric Egg Scrambler.

THE FIGHT

Our ingenious hero is locked in a room with Thomas Edison, a paper clip, a doggie toy, and a strawberry. This would be more than enough for him to work with, but each item has AC current surging through it, and MacGyver is electrocuted instantly.

THE WINNER

THOMAS EDISON (KO)

GANDALF

ALLIES: The Hobbits of Middle Earth; every dork in the universe

ENEMIES: Sauron; Saruman; folks who might be a bit sick of hearing about the Tower of Orthanc and the Kingdom of Rohan

OCCUPATION: Wizard

APPEARANCE: Wizardly, with the big beard and cloak

CHARACTERISTICS: Kind, wise gay guy

WHY HE'S GAY: First off, there's McKellen, who's great but gay as the day is long. Second, there's a weird NAMBLA-ish feel to his relationship with Frodo. Mostly, though, I just want to piss off *Lord of the Rings* fans.

SECRET HE CAN'T REVEAL: He totally wants to gay it up and gay it out with Frodo.

STRUGGLE AT THE HEART OF HIS EXISTENCE: The corruptible nature of incredible power

OBI-WAN KENOBI

ALLIES: Yoda; the Jedi Council

ENEMIES: Darth Maul; Anakin Skywalker when he goes bad

OCCUPATION: Jedi Master, which is much like Wizard, minus the emotional attachments

APPEARANCE: Wizardish as an older cat, though the beard is well trimmed. As a young man, a lot of people thought he looked like Ewan McGregor.

CHARACTERISTICS: Kind, wise hologram

SECRET HE CAN'T REVEAL: Darth Vader is Luke Skywalker's father.

STRUGGLE AT THE HEART OF HIS EXISTENCE: The corruptible nature of incredible power

MAGIC: He calls it The Force, which is kind of like when magicians call themselves illusionists.

HOMETOWN: Coruscant

PROBLEM: Going up against the greatest villain ever with Mark Hamill and a glowstick

GANDALF

MAGIC: He makes it happen like he's me with a lovely lady on the couch and D'Angelo on the stereo.

HOMETOWN: Valinor

A LITTLE TIP: Sci-fi girls dig it if you call them "my precious."

TRANSFORMATION: He "dies," his spirit travels out of time, he gets resurrected as Gandalf the White.

LOTR EFFECT ON MY BATHROOM BREAKS: Renaming feces "Radogast the Brown"

LOTR EFFECT ON MY MASTURBATION BREAKS: Now referred to as "scaling Mount Doom"

OBI-WAN KENOBI

STAR WARS EFFECT ON MY ELEMENTARY SCHOOL EXPERIENCE #1: Pretending to summon The Force through sipping from a Juicy Juice box

STAR WARS EFFECT ON MY ELEMENTARY SCHOOL EXPERIENCE #2: Talking like Yoda, but with lots of curses

TRANSFORMATION: He becomes one with The Force.

DISCLAIMER: He had nothing to do with Jar Jar Binks or casting the worst child actor ever as young Anakin Skywalker.

IN DEFENSE OF HIS BIGGEST FUCKUP: Sure he should have finished off Anakin when he had the chance. But then there would have been no Darth Vader, and hence no *Star Wars*. Do you like your action figures, lunch box, and blanket?

EXPERT ANALYSIS

"The mind boggles even trying to imagine a Kenobi vs. Gandalf scenario, although no doubt millions of unlicensed fanfics on the subject are currently eating the Internet. Let's dispense with the backstory and just assume that the New Republic is trying to colonize Middle Earth, and there's been a really gigantic misunderstanding along the way. So . . . Gandalf has untold wisdom, gadget-free magic, and a backup team of daring adventurers from different walks of life. Obi-Wan Kenobi—young Episode I–II version—has a light saber and a whiny apprentice. Obi-Wan Kenobi—classic 'Old Ben' version— has a . . . dang. But come on. Obi-Wan Kenobi is a freaking JEDI!"

—Dale Dobson, humorist for *Cracked,
National Lampoon,* and *Yankee Pot
Roast,* who will always be ten years old
when it comes to *Star Wars*

"Obi-Wan might not come out on top in a brawl with Gandalf, but he would still win, *from a certain point of view;* he knows that there are alternatives to fighting, and if you strike him down, he shall become more powerful than you can possibly imagine!"

—Evan "Rainbow Droideka" Centanni,
webmaster of the
www.yodasdatapad.com
Star Wars site

THE FIGHT

Judges do not permit either man to fight as an apparition, which severely changes their strategies. Also, no sudden magical disappearances allowed, a ruling both wizards protest. In the end, it is a straightforward swordfight, and Obi-Wan's superior weaponry and deft command of The Force lead him to a split decision over Gandalf in a disappointingly inactive battle characterized by both men spending a lot of time trying to conjure things and not much time actually fighting.

THE WINNER

OBI-WAN KENOBI (SPLIT DECISION)

SLEEP SCUFFLE

INSOMNIAC
vs.
NARCOLEPTIC

INSOMNIAC

ALLIES: Sleeping-pill manufacturers; early-morning infomercial stars; twenty-four-hour diner owners

ENEMIES: His bosses; coworkers; loved ones

TRIGGERS: Fear; stress; anxiety; doing lots of blow right before bedtime

ABILITY: Hallucinating without having to shell out for LSD

CHARACTERISTICS: Often manic, or depressive, or manic-depressive

FAVORITE MOVIE: *Taxi Driver*

TRADEMARK FIGHTING MOVE: The 5 A.M. Sneak Attack

TREATMENT: Benzodiazepines, which go great with tequila shots

REMEDIES FOR INSOMNIA: Afternoon exercise; early-evening bubble bath; warm milk before bedtime; smashing his head against his bedroom wall until he passes out

NARCOLEPTIC

ALLIES: "Friends" who ask him to fall asleep again, but do it better this time

ENEMIES: Lovers who can get a bit offended by inopportunely timed naps

SYMPTOM: Tendency to pass out suddenly, sometimes right before finishing a senten

COOL TRICK: Passing out into mashed potatoes

UNCOOL TRICK: Passing out on subway platform, into tracks

TRADEMARK FIGHTING MOVE: The Power Nap

FAVORITE MOVIE: *My Own Private Idaho*

TREATMENTS: Stimulants, although self-prescribing meth is a bad idea, believe you me

POOR CAREER CHOICES: Soldier; fireman; tightrope walker

THE FIGHT

The Narcoleptic is able to dodge the Insomniac's punches by passing out and falling on his face, a tactic that yields mixed results. The Insomniac, furious and delusional, shoots the Narcoleptic a hundred times before turning his gun on the ghosts in the room, which are making fun of him.

THE WINNER

INSOMNIAC (KO)

DREAM AND REALITY THROWDOWN

PASSION FRUIT

VS.

SIT AT HOME AND MASTURBATE FRUIT

PASSION FRUIT

FAMILY: Passifloraceae

JUICE: Very sweet and aromatic

SEEDS: Plentiful in its interior

EXTERIOR: The Golden Passion Fruit is bright yellow, smooth, and can be as large as a grapefruit. The dark purple passion fruit is smaller than a lemon and has a wrinkled rind.

ALLIES: Guava; pineapple

ENEMIES: Apple; peach

USES: Eaten fresh; used in fruit drinks as a syrup mixed with water and/or ice; added to other juice to make it sweeter and smell better; used as a topping on cakes

ALSO CALLED: Grenadilla; lilikoi

HOW IT GOT ITS NAME: The fruit's flower reminded early European explorers of symbols associated with the Passion of Christ.

SIT AT HOME AND MASTURBATE FRUIT

FAMILY: Extremely ashamed

JUICE: Squirted all over its skin

SEEDS: Plentiful on its bed and recliner

EXTERIOR: Unkempt, stained, smelling distinctly of a mixture of bodily functions

ALLIES: Onanistic Orange; Perverted Pear

ENEMIES: Moralistic Mango; Prudish Papaya

USES: Completely useless

ALSO CALLED: Waste of Space Fruit; Get Off Your Ass and Do Something Fruit

HOW IT GOT ITS NAME: By watching *Dirty Debutantes 1–53* in a single week

THE FIGHT

Passion Fruit is bursting with excitement for this battle but is horrified by one look at Sit at Home and Masturbate Fruit's bathroom floor, which is covered with dustballs, dirt, mold, urine, traces of feces, and Betty Crocker vanilla icing. SAHAM Fruit uses this shell shock to his advantage, beating Passion Fruit to a (delicious) pulp with a battle-axe composed completely of old, stuck-together copies of *Hustler.*

THE WINNER

SIT AT HOME AND MASTURBATE FRUIT (KO)

PHILOSOPHER/ROBOT BATTLE

VOLTAIRE
vs.
VOLTRON

VOLTAIRE

ALLIES: Champions of reason; dudes trying to look smart in cafés

ENEMIES: The Aristocracy; Royalty; Gottfried Leibniz, a German mathematician and philosopher who unfortunately died before he and Voltaire could have a steel cage match

VIEWS ON RELIGION: Deist who rejected Christianity and whose belief in God was based on reason rather than faith

OPPOSED TO: The hypocrisies and injustices of the French Enlightenment establishment

VOLTAIRE ACTION FIGURE: Sits down, rubs temples, jots notes

GIVEN NAME: François-Marie Arouet

INFLUENCES: John Locke; Isaac Newton; Scott Baio; Kirk Cameron

OCCUPATIONS: Essayist/novelist/poet/philosopher

LOVE INTEREST: The Marquise du Châtelet

VOLTRON

ALLIES: Space Mice; Princess Romelle; King Alfor

ENEMIES: King Zarkon; Prince Lotor; Haggar; Yurak; various Robeasts

VIEWS ON RELIGION: *Deus ex machina*

OPPOSED TO: The hypocrisies and injustices of Gobots, Transformers

VOLTRON ACTION FIGURE: There was an action figure?

INFLUENCES: Anime series *Golion* and *Dairugger XV*

OCCUPATIONS: Robot Lions; Aqua Fighters; Turbo Terrain Fighters; Strato Fighters

LOVE INTERESTS: A toaster and a VCR

SAD TRUTH: Guys who couldn't get their GEDs or name their senator can identify hundreds of made-up cartoon robots.

CORRESPONDENCE: Many text messages sent from its arms to its legs

VOLTAIRE

CORRESPONDENCE: Wrote over 21,000 letters, most claiming to be a Nigerian general looking to send you gold in exchange for a small donation.

WEAPON: The pen, which isn't as mighty as all that.

TRADEMARK FIGHTING MOVES: The Aphorism Leglock; The Pile Driver of Irony

HIS MOST FAMOUS WORK: *Candide,* followed closely by *He's Just Not That Into You*

CHURCH AND STATE: Should be separate.

OUTPUT: Extremely prolific, publishing a plethora of plays, novels, poems, histories, philosophical works, energy drinks, and microwavable popcorns

VOLTAIRE FORCE: Philosophy majors; French lit students

MEMORABLE QUOTES: "If God did not exist it would be necessary to invent him"; "I've got an appetite for love 'cause me so horny."

VOLTRON

DIFFERENCES BETWEEN THE JAPANESE AND AMERICAN SERIES: The American series is less violent, but more obese and worse on standardized tests.

CHURCH AND STATE: Should join together like a giant mecha robot.

OUTPUTS: Multiple, with many inputs as well

ORIGIN: Originally a unified machine that was blown into five pieces, which became the five lions.

VOLTRON FORCE: Commander Keith Akira Kogane; Lance Charles McClain; Pidge Stoker

MOVIE: Set for 2008 release, starring Meryl Streep and Dame Judi Dench in Oscar-worthy performances as the Red Lion and the Green Lion.

EXPERT ANALYSIS

"The 18th-century philosopher and essayist seems no match for the united force of the mighty Voltron, Defender of the Universe. In a desperate pinch, Voltaire's admiration of Isaac Newton might give him an edge if he could convince Voltron that physics make his most awesome '80's moves impossible. If he could then somehow apply magical or nuclear power to the work of his predecessor Descartes, he could summon the Cartesian demon to distract Voltron, then use Cartesian coordinates to translate himself the hell out of harm's way. But these fanciful applications of Voltaire's knowledge seem highly unlikely to work out."

—Dale Dobson, humorist for *Cracked, National Lampoon,* and *Yankee Pot Roast*

"Voltaire believed that the ideal form of government was 'enlightened despotism'—a society ruled by an absolute monarch taking advice from philosophers. Democracy was but 'the idiocy of the masses,' and, in fact, he was horrified by the 'hordes' of common people. Opponent Voltron is a shape-changing giant mecha robot. In his first incarnation as 'Lion Voltron,' he consists of five robot lions commanded by five intrepid young pilots, combined into a unified machine intelligence capable of defending planet Arus from evil king Zarkon. If Voltaire was afraid of French peasants, what the hell is he going to do about that? Winner: Voltron."

—Jennifer Dzuria, stand-up comedienne, blogger (www.jenisfamous.com)

"Voltaire wrote, 'Meditation is the dissolution of thoughts in eternal awareness or pure consciousness without objectification, knowing without thinking, merging finitude in infinity.' I hope it provides him with some small consolation before Voltron splits him in two with his blazing sword."

—Dave Itzkoff, science fiction book reviewer, *New York Times Book Review,* author of *Lads: A Memoir of Manhood*

"On one end of the battlefield we have a shape-changing robotic monstrosity the size of a building, composed of car-sized robotic jungle animals and swinging a glowing energy sword. On the other end, we have a poofy philosopher sitting in front of a Victorian-era rolltop desk holding a quill pen. Clearly, Voltaire is laser-bait—so long as mighty Voltron avoids being drawn into a head-bursting philosophical discussion on the meaning of life, death, and freedom."

—Daniel Wilson, author, *How to Survive a Robot Uprising* and *How to Build a Robot Army*

THE FIGHT

The French philosopher seems over-matched against the shape-changing robot, but Mecha-Voltaire is another story! A robotic, superpowered version of the influential thinker wisely joins forces with Mecha-Descartes, Mecha-Camus, Mecha-Sartre, and Mecha-Derrida to create a giant ass-kicking French Philosopher Robot that immobilizes Voltron with an energy field of reason and logic, before deconstructing him with a laser of analysis.

THE WINNER

VOLTAIRE (KO)

ALL-TIME

COMBATANT
RANKINGS

GENIUSES

1. Albert Einstein
2. Sir Isaac Newton
3. Leonardo da Vinci
4. Bill Belichick
5. Thomas Edison
6. Srinivasa Ramanujan
7. Mozart
8. Marie Curie
9. Galileo Galilei
10. Ron Popeil

GAYS

1. Michelangelo
2. Portia de Rossi
3. Leonardo da Vinci
4. Plato
5. JM J. Bullock
6. Langston Hughes
7. Caravaggio
8. Sappho
9. Oscar Wilde
10. Ted Allen, the food queer from *Queer Eye for the Straight Guy*

GREAT BEASTS

1. Leviathan
2. King Kong
3. Chupacabra
4. Kraken
5. Godzilla
6. Mothra
7. Scylla
8. Charybdis
9. Loch Ness Monster
10. Mike Tyson

HOT WOMEN BORN BEFORE 1975

1. Salma Hayek
2. Halle Berry
3. Sarah Silverman
4. Winona Ryder
5. Padma Lakshmi
6. Rachel Weisz
7. Famke Janssen
8. Lucy Liu
9. Gwen Stefani
10. Kate Moss

HOT WOMEN BORN IN 1975

1. Angelina Jolie
2. Eva Longoria
3. Natalie Imbruglia
4. Kate Winslet
5. Milla Jovovich
6. Asia Argento
7. Drew Barrymore
8. Charlize Theron
9. Chelsea Handler
10. Lauryn Hill
11. Mia Kirshner
12. Kimora Lee Simmons
13. Tara Reid
14. Niki Taylor
15. Scary Spice
16. Alicia Witt
17. Kylie Bax
18. Linda Cardellini
19. Jolene Blalock
20. Danica McKellar

HOT WOMEN BORN 1976–82

1. Rosario Dawson
2. Natalie Portman
3. Jessica Alba
4. Zooey Deschanel
5. Jennifer Carpenter
6. Zhang Ziyi
7. Katherine Heigl
8. Maggie Gyllenhaal
9. Jessica Biel
10. Beyoncé Knowles

HOT WOMEN BORN 1983–1989

1. Scarlett Johansson
2. Megan Fox
3. Keira Knightley
4. Mila Kunis
5. Lindsay Lohan
6. Maria Sharapova
7. Joss Stone
8. Katherine McPhee
9. Michelle Trachtenberg
10. Mischa Barton

HOT WOMEN BORN AFTER 1990*

ROBOTS

1. The Terminator
2. Bender
3. R2-D2
4. The Iron Giant
5. Johnny 5
6. HAL 9000
7. Optimus Prime
8. C-3PO
9. Dick Cheney
10. Robby the Robot

MONKEYS

1. King Kong
2. Cornelius
3. Koko
4. Curious George
5. Donkey Kong

*Censored due to ongoing *Dateline NBC* investigation of Jake Kalish

6. Magilla Gorilla
7. Clyde
8. Dr. Zaius
9. Bubbles
10. Marcel

JEWS

1. Sandy Koufax
2. Jesus
3. Scarlett Johansson
   (Her mom's a Jew, so
   she counts.)
4. Albert Einstein
5. Bob Dylan (conversion or no)
6. Mel Brooks
7. Philip Roth
8. Moses
9. Sigmund Freud
10. Jonas Salk
11. Groucho Marx
12. Karl Marx
13. Gilda Radner
14. Franz Kafka
15. Woody Allen
16. Arthur Miller
17. Dustin Hoffman
18. Paul Simon
19. Captain Kirk and Mr. Spock
20. Natalie Portman and Winona
    Ryder and Rachel Weisz and
    Sarah Silverman

BLACKS

1. Jesus
2. Muhammad Ali
3. Martin Luther King
4. Louis Armstrong
5. Richard Pryor

6. Halle Berry
7. Nelson Mandela
8. Michael Jordan
9. Eddie Murphy
10. Luke "Power Man" Cage

ASIANS

1. Bruce Lee
2. Buddha
3. Gandhi
4. Akira Kurosawa
5. Confucius
6. Lucy Liu
7. The Dalai Lama
8. Genghis Khan
9. Lao-tzu
10. Yao Ming

LATINOS

1. Rosario Dawson
2. Gabriel Garcia Márquez
3. Pedro Martinez
4. Salma Hayek
5. Eva Mendes
6. Jennifer Lopez
7. Mario Vargas Llosa
8. César Chávez
9. Shakira
10. Johan Santana

BLIND PEOPLE

1. Daredevil
2. Ray Charles
3. Homer
4. Stevie Wonder
5. John Milton
6. Art Tatum

7. Helen Keller
8. Blind Lemon Jefferson
9. Louis Braille
10. Clarence Carter

LITTLE PEOPLE

1. Bushwick Bill
2. Toulouse-Lautrec
3. Bridget the Midget
4. Tony Cox
5. Hervé Villechaize
6. Gary Coleman
7. Verne Troyer
8. Wee-Man
9. Warwick Davis
10. Billy Barty

ASSHOLES

1. Adolf Hitler
2. Barry Bonds
3. Johnny Lawrence, the blond asshole from *The Karate Kid*
4. Osama Bin Laden
5. Nurse Ratched
6. Dick Cheney
7. Joseph McCarthy
8. Gargamel
9. Donald Trump
10. J. Jonah Jameson

ALCOHOLICS

1. André the Giant (Once drank a *case* of wine in a day.)
2. Judy Garland
3. Boris Yeltsin
4. Dean Martin
5. Barney Gumble

6. John Daly
7. Jim Morrison
8. Raymond Carver
9. Billie Holiday (A better junkie than alcoholic.)
10. Amy Winehouse (All she lacks is experience.)

DRUG ADDICTS

1. Keith Richards
2. Charlie Parker
3. John Belushi
4. Billie Holiday
5. Sigmund Freud
6. Darryl Strawberry and Dwight Gooden
7. Kurt Cobain
8. Anna Nicole Smith
9. Ozzy Osbourne
10. Sherlock Holmes

PROPHETS

1. Miss Cleo
2. Moses
3. L. Ron Hubbard
4. Jesus (Yeah, yeah, argue it up.)
5. Muhammad
6. Joseph Smith
7. Abraham
8. David Koresh
9. Menachem Schneerson
10. Nostradamus

BATSHIT CRAZY PEOPLE

1. That batshit crazy little Iranian dictator
2. Vincent Van Gogh
3. George Clinton
4. Steve-O
5. Wesley Willis
6. Son of Sam
7. My friend Dan T.
8. Crispin Glover
9. Courtney Love
10. GG Allin

MARVEL SUPERHEROES

1. Daredevil
2. Silver Surfer
3. Spider-Man
4. Power Man and Iron Fist
5. Rogue
6. The Hulk
7. Wolverine
8. Thor
9. Beast
10. The Punisher

DC SUPERHEROES

1. Batman
2. Green Lantern
3. The Flash
4. Aquaman
5. Wonder Woman
6. Catwoman
7. Green Arrow
8. Plastic Man
9. Firestorm
10. Superman (I'm sorry, but his weakness is some stupid stone that's not native to Earth and his disguise is a pair of glasses.)

PEANUTS CHARACTERS

1. Charlie Brown
2. Linus
3. The Little Red-Haired Girl (*especially* because you never saw her)
4. Snoopy
5. Pigpen
6. Schroeder
7. Lucy
8. Peppermint Patty
9. Sally
10. Joe Shlabotnik

SIMPSONS CHARACTERS

1. Apu
2. Moe
3. Ralph Wiggum
4. Homer
5. Bart
6. Mr. Burns
7. Crusty
8. Lisa
9. Marge
10. Selma and Patty

WRESTLING HEELS

1. Rowdy Roddy Piper
2. Randy "Macho Man" Savage
3. The Iron Sheik
4. Andy Kaufman
5. Ravishing Rick Rude
6. Triple H

7. Vince McMahon
8. King Kong Bundy
9. Ted "The Million Dollar Man" DiBiase
10. Bobby "The Brain" Heenan

PEOPLE TO PRETEND TO KNOW ABOUT IN INTELLIGENT CONVERSATION

1. Jacques Derrida
2. Marshall McLuhan
3. Martin Heidegger
4. Noam Chomsky
5. Andrei Tarkovsky
6. Harold Bloom
7. Sergei Eisenstein
8. Jacques Lacan
9. Howard Zinn
10. Michel Foucault

SEXUAL POSITIONS IN THE KAMA SUTRA

1. Congress of a Crow
2. The Splitting of a Bamboo
3. The Elephant Posture
4. The Lotus Position
5. The Pair of Tongs
6. The Crab's Position
7. The Encircling Position
8. The Fixing of a Nail
9. The Longbow
10. The Concealed Door

JACK NICHOLSON ROLES

1. Randle P. McMurphy in *One Flew Over the Cuckoo's Nest*
2. Jack Torrance in *The Shining*
3. Jake Gittes in *Chinatown*
4. Melvin Udall in *As Good As It Gets*
5. The Joker in *Batman*
6. Garrett Breedlove in *Terms of Endearment*
7. Warren Schmidt in *About Schmidt*
8. Col. Jessup in *A Few Good Men*
9. Charley Partanna in *Prizzi's Honor*
10. George Hanson in *Easy Rider*

ROBERT DE NIRO ROLES

1. Travis Bickle in *Taxi Driver*
2. Jake LaMotta in *Raging Bull*
3. Young Vito Corleone in *The Godfather Part II*
4. Jimmy Conway in *Goodfellas*
5. Max Cady in *Cape Fear*
6. Rupert Pipkin in *The King of Comedy*
7. Al Capone in *The Untouchables*
8. Jack Walsh in *Midnight Run*
9. Sam Rothstein in *Casino*
10. Johnny Boy Civello in *Mean Streets*

DUSTIN HOFFMAN ROLES

1. Benjamin Braddock in *The Graduate*
2. Ratso Rizzo in *Midnight Cowboy*
3. Michael Dorsey and Dorothy Michaels in *Tootsie*
4. Raymond Babbitt in *Rain Man*
5. Ted Kramer in *Kramer vs. Kramer*
6. Lenny Bruce in *Lenny*
7. David Summer in *Straw Dogs*
8. Thomas Levy in *Marathon Man*
9. Louis Dega in *Papillon*
10. Jack Crabb in *Little Big Man*

POKER PLAYERS

1. Doyle Brunson (until the day he dies)
2. Phil Ivey
3. Allen Cunningham
4. Dan Harrington
5. Ted Forrest
6. Phil Hellmuth
7. Daniel Negreanu
8. Chris "Jesus" Ferguson
9. John Juanda
10. Gus Hansen
11. Scotty Nguyen
12. Barry Greenstein
13. Johnny Chan
14. Erik Seidel
15. Antonio Esfandiari
16. Mike Sexton
17. Erick Lindgren
18. Annie Duke
19. Carlos Mortensen
20. Phil Laak

TV COPS/DETECTIVES

1. David Caruso as Lt. John Kelly on *NYPD Blue*
2. Leslie Nielsen as Det. Frank Drebin on *Police Squad!*
3. Bruce Willis and Cybill Shepherd as David Addison and Maddie Hayes on *Moonlighting*
4. Dominic West as Det. Jimmy McNulty on *The Wire*
5. Farrah Fawcett as Jill Munroe on *Charlie's Angels*
6. Peter Falk as Lt. Columbo on *Columbo*
7. Hal Linden as Barney Miller on *Barney Miller*
8. Don Johnson and Phillip Michael Thomas as Sonny Crockett and Ricardo Tubbs on *Miami Vice*
9. Tom Selleck as Thomas Magnum on *Magnum P.I.*
10. Jerry Orbach as Det. Lennie Briscoe on *Law & Order*

TV DOCTORS

1. Alan Alda as Hawkeye Pierce on *M*A*S*H*
2. Rob Morrow as Joel Fleischman on *Northern Exposure*
3. George Clooney as Doug Ross on *ER*
4. Bill Cosby as Cliff Huxtable on *The Cosby Show*

5. Hugh Laurie as Gregory House on *House*
6. Zack Braff as J. D. Dorian on *Scrubs*
7. Neil Patrick Harris as Doogie Howser on *Doogie Howser, M.D.*
8. Denzel Washington as Dr. Philip Chandler on *St. Elsewhere*
9. Jane Seymour as Michaela Quinn on *Dr. Quinn, Medicine Woman*
10. Katherine Heigl as Izzie Stevens on *Grey's Anatomy*

TV LAWYERS

1. John Larroquette as Dan Fielding on *Night Court*
2. Sam Waterston as Jack McCoy on *Law & Order*
3. Calista Flockhart as Ally McBeal and Peter McNichol as John Cage on *Ally McBeal*
4. Dylan McDermott as Bobby Donnell on *The Practice*
5. Tom Cavanagh as Ed Stevens on *Ed*
6. Phil Hartman as Caveman Lawyer on *Saturday Night Live*
7. Corbin Bernsen as Arnie Becker on *LA Law*
8. Andy Griffith as Matlock on *Matlock*
9. Eric McCormack as Will Truman on *Will & Grace*
10. Raymond Burr as Perry Mason on *Perry Mason*

FAT PEOPLE

1. Buddha
2. Eric Cartman
3. John Belushi
4. Tony Soprano
5. Old Elvis
6. Chris Farley
7. Santa Claus
8. Jackie Gleason
9. Winston Churchill
10. Fat Albert

SKINNY PEOPLE

1. Mick Jagger
2. Jesus
3. Angelina Jolie
4. Keira Knightley
5. David Bowie
6. Ric Ocasek
7. Nicole Richie
8. Mary-Kate and Ashley Olsen
9. Calista Flockhart
10. Kate Moss

PEOPLE WHO KILLED THEMSELVES

1. Romeo and Juliet
2. Vincent Van Gogh
3. Ernest Hemingway
4. Willy Loman
5. Kurt Cobain
6. Marilyn Monroe
7. Seymour Glass
8. Ophelia
9. Yukio Mishima
10. John Kennedy Toole

MURDERED PEOPLE

1. Jesus
2. Hamlet
3. Abraham Lincoln
4. Martin Luther King, Jr.
5. John F. Kennedy
6. Malcolm X
7. John Lennon
8. Marvin Gaye
9. Biggie and Tupac
10. Julius Caesar

ANIMALS THAT EAT FECES

1. Pigs
2. Dogs
3. Naked Mole Rats
4. Rabbits
5. Pandas
6. Elephants
7. Hippos
8. Gorillas
9. Hamsters
10. George "The Animal" Steele

BALD PEOPLE

1. Charlie Brown
2. Pablo Picasso
3. Michael Jordan
4. Gandhi
5. George Costanza
6. Sinead O'Connor
7. Homer Simpson
8. Hippocrates
9. Rob Reiner
10. Lex Luthor
11. Andre Agassi
12. Dwight D. Eisenhower
13. Ron Howard
14. Patrick Stewart
15. Kareem Abdul-Jabbar
16. Kojak
17. Peter Gabriel
18. George Foreman
19. Bruce Willis
20. Hulk Hogan

SOCIOCULTURAL SIGNIFICANCE OF THESE ★IMAGINED ALTERCATIONS

THE ONE YOU LOVE VS. THE ONE YOU'RE WITH

Have you ever heard a man try to claim the one girl who'd have him is the girl of his dreams? It's sad to behold, but it makes for some unbelievable justifications.

BILL BUCKNER VS. THE BALL THAT WENT BETWEEN HIS LEGS

Who among us hasn't fucked up? And I mean *royally* fucked up, fucked up big, fucked up so bad just thinking about it makes you shake, shudder, and want to smack the memory clear out of your head forever? Who among us hasn't had their Buckner moment? I haven't. Never made a mistake in my life. Don't know what that's about.

ADAM VS. CHARLES DARWIN

We go back and forth in this country, faith battling reason, the endless argument over Intelligent Design. Scientists try to explain that what they mean by "theory"—i.e., something with overwhelming evidence that has not (and likely cannot) be *completely* proven without a shadow of a doubt—is not the same as what Born-Again Bill calls a theory—i.e., something he heard someone say on Sunday-morning television. Intelligent Design advocates point to the strength of their primary source—you know, Jehovah, yahweh, the Big G_d. (Also, their story is better—they've got villains, a tragic figure, adventure, a snake. Darwin's got a monkey and a chart.) We won't get anywhere talking about this. This needs to be solved Old West–style, mano–a–first mano, the guy who fell from paradise and the dude who rose from apes. Winner decides where we came from.

SANTA VS. SATAN

Same guy, different climate.

THE LUCKY VS. THE SKILLED

This guy I know is a favorite in roulette every time he picks a number. A hundred bucks on number ten, number ten it is. Three times in a row. He makes every stupid sucker bet in the house, and they all come in. I study what games to play and how best to beat them, and wind up pawning my watch and borrowing bus fare home.

MY DAD VS. YOUR DAD

If imaginary fighting were an academic discipline, this would be the introductory course, and on the first day students would be required to list ten ways in which their father was better than, and would kick the ass of, the father of the student sitting next to them. Anyone with a complete wuss for a father would have to detail ten ways in which their father was wussish, and if these were deemed acceptable, could substitute "brother," "uncle," or, if raised in a sapphic household, "second mother" for father in their lists.

THE VIRGIN VS. THE WHORE

If you ever attended high school, you already know all about this.

THAT PERVY GUY YOU HEARD ABOUT WITH THE FUNNY THING STUCK IN HIS ASS WHO HAD TO GO TO THE DOCTOR VS. THAT PERVY GIRL WITH THE FUNNY THING STUCK IN HER PUSSY WHO HAD TO GO TO THE DOCTOR

Generally, the funny thing was a live animal of some sort, although occasionally it was a large phallic vegetable, foot-long hot dog, Tonka truck, or action figure. Another favorite character was the guy or girl who got caught by their parents having sex with their pet, sometimes because they got their business stuck in the pet's hoo-ha, or the other way around. Regardless, neither held a candle to the male rock star who had to have his stomach pumped of a gallon of cum. A gallon, I swear. At *least* a gallon.

STORK VS. GRIM REAPER

The first thing I'm going to do when I have a kid, just as soon as he's old enough, is sit him down on my lap and explain that the clock is ticking and he's already begun the slow descent to death and nothingness. That should put things into perspective for the kid and make dopey questions like "Where do babies come from?" seem a little less important.

SELF-HELP GURU VS. FAILURE

Apparently, all you have to do to achieve success is visualize it. If you can dream it, you can do it. Hold on, I'm dreaming. Nope, still not pitching for the Mets. Maybe I'm getting bad reception on my dream. I'll switch the channel. One moment, please. No, that's still my own hand down there on my joint, definitely not Scarlett Johansson's. Hers would be less hairy.

THE LESBIAN OF YOUR LESBIAN PORNO VS. THE LESBIAN OF YOUR FOURTH-PERIOD GYM CLASS

Too many of us have spent our lives as monkeys in the middle, tennis balls of opportunity hopelessly whizzing above our heads. I, for one, vow to catch that ball and escape the middle. I will be the monkey with the ball.

EUROPEAN DRAGON VS. ASIAN DRAGON

The cultural and economic battle between the Eastern and Western world will, in many ways, define this upcoming century. This is not that battle. But it has dragons.

This is an actual argument friends of mine engage in ferociously while their rooms go uncleaned and their rent goes unpaid. I love my friends.

BARBIE VS. KEN

The cultural significance of Barbie can't be overstated. She's most little girls' first chance to discover what it means to be a woman. (That is, until they sleep with me.) In this role, Barbie has been cursed by her overwhelming popularity—there wouldn't be a plethora of angry feminist diatribes about her tiny waist and giant knockers if fourteen kids in Omaha owned the doll. Ken has not been similarly demonized, because he supposedly poses no threat to anyone, doing whatever his love says, following her everywhere. No threat? Really? My first girlfriend tried to twist my head around, move my arms, and dress me in hot pants. She was surprised I actually had genitals. (Very pleasantly surprised, might I add.) Of course, Barbie and Ken give young girls the completely wrong idea of what men and women are, and how they relate to each other. So fucking what? The fact is, little kids need fantasy, and it's awfully presumptuous of us old, broken adults to dictate exactly what those fantasies should be. Are our female dolls supposed to look like Rosie O'Donnell? Should our male dolls behave like Ike Turner? Come to think of it, yes. That would be kind of excellent.

MARRIED GAY COUPLE VS. DIVORCED STRAIGHT COUPLE

How we doing as a society? Really great? Everyone's happy and everything's perfect? If not, if we have legitimate problems—like, for example, we're in an unwinnable war, the rest of the world really isn't digging us, we're poorly educated, have a disastrous health-care system, are in constant debt, and don't seem to give a shit about poor black folks drowning to death—then maybe we can lay off people who love each other, even if that love is hot pink and unbiblical.

DUNGEONS AND DRAGONS PLAYERS VS. WORLD OF WARCRAFT PLAYERS

We're living in a charmed era for dorks. The world has a gigantic hard-on for the Internet, virtual realities abound, and many of the biggest games, books, and movies are wizard-driven. Now, at the very least, you have to wait until the dork fixes your hard drive and gives you video game cheat codes before you hit him with the wedgie-swirlie combo.

CONSPIRACY THEORISTS VS. CONSPIRATORS

The most fun thing about arguing with conspiracy theorists is that the more evidence you present that, say, Al Qaeda might have been responsible for 9/11 and, you know, Oswald was the lone gunman, the more they look at you with those condescending eyes, nod their heads, and smile at you like you're the biggest sucker in the world for believing "credible sources." Wait, that's not fun, it's horribly unpleasant. My mistake.

MUHAMMAD ALI VS. BRUCE LEE

Lee vs. Ali was my introduction to the topic of imaginary fights in elementary school. My Dad vs. Your Dad never really picked up steam, as many of my friends were little Chinese kids, with similarly little (but extremely hardworking) fathers. My dad could have eaten their dads alive, especially after their dads got off the fourteen-hour factory shift. No, this was our fight, between the two coolest guys ever: Eastern elegance and Western style. We had many theories, and analyzed this in depth. With boxing gloves or not? Three-minute rounds or last man standing? Kicking allowed? Nunchucks? (No nunchucks was generally the decision.) Mike Tyson also made an appearance in these imaginary battles, but it was nasty, brutish, and short, like Iron Mike himself. Usually Bruce Lee won, but that's what I get for going to elementary school in Chinatown.

HOLLYWOOD LIBERALS AND THE JEWISH MEDIA VS. HONEST, HARDWORKING AMERICANS

I'm a liberal, and a Jew, and a member of the media. (I just don't live in Hollywood.) Here's my question. If we're supposed to run everything, how come my bathroom is filthy and I had to borrow money last week?

THE ULTIMATE WARRIOR VS. THE ULTIMATE PACIFIST

It's possible this isn't the best book in which to seriously discuss the complex issue that is nonviolent resistance. With that in mind, I am hard at work on *The Official Compendium of Imaginary Protests.*

AUNT JEMIMA VS. UNCLE BEN

The whole race issue has taken a weird turn in this country. It used to be a forum for true greatness, real sacrifice, and heroism—MLK leading marches, Schwerner, Cheney, and Goodman fighting the good fight and dying together. Now, with less institutionalized racism, for some reason it seems like any discussion of race turns the person discussing it into a raging asshole. White, black, yellow, brown, doesn't matter, you're just a dick.

COMPULSIVE GAMBLER VS. RACEHORSE

I don't know a damn thing about compulsive gambling, and I certainly didn't just take a five-hour break to play Internet poker, which the United States government has made infinitely more difficult for people not at all like me, such that these people, whom I don't know and wouldn't associate with, have to get a prepaid credit card and request a check to get their earnings, which may or may not be $322.61, or so I have heard.

DONALD DUCK VS. DAFFY DUCK

The question of Daffy vs. Donald, and, by extension, Disney vs. Looney Tunes, is as clear a dividing line for the preadolescent boy as Marvel vs. DC (or Spider-Man/Superman), American vs. National League, the kids allowed to eat junk food and the kids who weren't. In short, these things defined who we were and how we saw the world. Kids who liked Disney cartoons gave hugs for no reason and believed everything would work out fine. Looney Tunes kids might hit you just for standing there, and were waiting for something else to go wrong.

Nothing truly awful ever happens in a Mickey Mouse or Donald Duck cartoon. The protagonists are adorable, and unlike either humans or their animal counterparts—Donald Duck isn't much like a person *or* a duck, but rather an idealized amalgamation designed to make the young, impressionable, and innocent believe in a better, kinder, more awww-inducing world, a smoothed-out utopia complete with hundred-dollar day passes, family packages, and must-have souvenirs. Sure, unlike Mickey, Donald gets angry and shouts and stomps a lot, but his fury seems random, undirected, like an adorable baby crying to be heard. On the other hand, characters in Looney Tunes cartoons have every reason to be upset. Anything that can go badly in Looney Tunes cartoons generally does, often in a spectacularly violent manner. They tell children a boulder *will* fall on your head. A bomb *will* go off in your face. You *will* step on a rake, over and over and over again. Unlike in the Disney Universe, heightened unreality exists not to mask the cruel underlying truth but to maximize its impact: You defy gravity just long enough to know you're about to fall, and wave good-bye. And the characters are *us*, in all our ugly pettiness, duplicity, jealousy, and frustration. Nowhere is this more apparent than in Daffy, who is Salieri to Bugs's Amadeus, Garfunkel to his Simon, Chasez to his Timberlake. Daffy's world is cruel and unjust, and he is wholly incapable of rising above it. He's for the kids whose parents yell too much, who get carob instead of chocolate, who know exactly which table is the cool table, and don't get to sit at it, and don't deserve to. God bless him for that.

THE CONSTIPATED VS. THE INCONTINENT

How come "anal retentive" made its way into the contemporary lexicon and "anal expulsive" didn't? I'm anal expulsive. I shit all over the place. I shat all over this book. Also, the expression "shit or get off the pot" strikes me as strange. Why would you be on the pot if you didn't intend to shit? Maybe you can't shit because some asshole is pressuring you. And that's the other thing—are we to understand there is someone waiting to use the pot, nearly bursting with shit, who is inconvenienced by this fecal dilly-dallying? Why does he or she give a shit if you shit? It's possible I'm thinking about this too literally.

DRUNK VS. STONER

Of course, the answer is no one wins, ever. And don't give me the horseshit artist excuse "Ernest Hemingway was an alcoholic," or "Bob Marley smoked weed every day of his life." You could guzzle bourbon straight from the bottle and suck on the bong until your lips bleed, you're not writing like Hemingway or singing like Marley. You're just going to vomit on the furniture or forget to go to work, and wonder why no one returns your phone calls.

PAC-MAN VS. MS. PAC-MAN

Ms. Pac-Man exemplifies the problems faced by a woman in the workforce: Though she may be smarter, faster, better, may work harder, might actually have *eyes*, in the end she is playing a game created by men for men. Unless the chicks make the rules, they'll always run into the Inkies and Blinkies of the patriarchy.

MANIC-DEPRESSIVES VS. OBSESSIVE-COMPULSIVES

Really, the answer should be whichever one will give me their pills first. Daddy needs to self-medicate.

CELEBRITY PUBLICISTS AND CELEBRITY ASSISTANTS VS. PAPARAZZI AND GOSSIP COLUMNISTS

Ah, fame. We can't get enough, and then we want to destroy it. I can make fun of Lindsay Lohan all I want, but I still know exactly what she did yesterday. She had sex with me and Paris Hilton. Oh, and Scarlett Johansson was there too. Plus, Lohan and Johansson don't get along, so there was a whole competitive element to the ménage à quatre that was ungodly hot.

ROBOT VS. BARBARIAN

This was, by far, the hardest call as to who would actually win the fight. I went back and forth many times. In truth, I'm still not completely sure. If anyone can actually make this fight happen—if, perhaps, you're a robotics professor who lives among cannibals—please do this and YouTube it for me.

COQUETTE VS. COKEHEAD

Neither one will probably be as into hanging with you once the bar closes. Well, that's not completely true. If it's a really dedicated, secretive cokehead with some bankroll, he can keep excusing himself to various bathrooms for days, months, even weeks, until he goes broke, gets intervened on, or has a heart attack.

KERMIT THE FROG AND MISS PIGGY VS. BERT AND ERNIE

If you look at all the original Muppets, they're weird. Insecure, easily annoyed, too passive or too aggressive, deluded, a bit crazy. And uniformly awesome. Certainly, these four are great. Adorable little Elmo, on the other hand, is bullshit.

PIRATE VS. NINJA

It's amazing to follow the train of thought on most Internet message boards. The third stop is invariably "U R a moron," followed by "U R a fag."

METROSEXUAL VS. EUNUCH

There is no cultural relevance to this. None whatsoever. I just felt Eunuchs needed a shout-out. God knows, it's the least we can do.

ARTIST VS. CRITIC

It's my duty as someone in a creative field to make fun of critics in some small way. It's a rite of passage. If they like this book, I will hug them all and marvel at their brilliance.

HE-MAN VS. SHE-MALES

Not every mensch can be an übermensch—in fact, some mensches don't want to be mensches at all. As He-Man epitomizes everything great, powerful, and heroic in the male gender, so the She-Male defies these same ideals, and uses silicone, makeup, and hormone treatments to create, as if by magic, a choice C in an A and B equation—a boobermensch, if you will. And yet, both are somehow all they can be. As He-Man lifts his sword to the sky and boldly summons the Power of Grayskull, the She-Male tucks hers (his? hers?) back in the lace panties, a secret shame, a topic of some awfully confusing and somewhat traumatizing late-night drunken conversation when I really should have noticed the size of those hands, and the fact that both condoms couldn't have been for me.

NECROPHILIAC VS. GHOST OF THE DEAD WOMAN HE'S SCREWING

There are no victimless crimes.

SAMURAI VS. GLADIATOR

Everything everyone does should be subject to a code of honor, and there should be consequences for breaking that code. Cockblock your friend? You're forced to do battle unto death. Steal someone's idea and use it as your own? Get attacked by a dude with a sword. Fuck over your family? Get attacked by a lion. There should be *many* scenarios wherein assholes get attacked by lions.

MICHAEL CORLEONE VS. TONY MONTANA

This is a classic battle of alpha male opposites—the watcher vs. the talker, the quiet panther and the roaring lion, both poised to pounce at any moment. Panthers are quiet, right? I grew up in New York City. Fuck if I know.

SCIENTIST VS. SCIENTOLOGIST

As goofy as all this Scientology shit is (and it's awful goofy), Cruise, Travolta, Beck, Isaac Hayes, and the rest of them are really cursed by when their religion came to be and how easily one can trace its origin. If some crappy sci-fi author came up with a dude parting a sea or a virgin giving birth, we'd be yukking it up about that, too.

BARNEY VS. GRIMACE

Fucking Barney. We want our children to be happy, but not if this is the price we pay. That is one insidiously giddy purple fucking dinosaur. And forget about Grimace and the rest of the evil McDonald's crew. Can I have a mutated chicken dipped in lard, please? Can you stick some bread between two beef-and-dryer-lint patties? That's brilliant. (Can McDonald's help promote this book? I love McDonald's.)

I actually do dig McNuggets, Quarter Pounders with Cheese, and various selections from the 99-cent menu, but that doesn't mean I can't get a little self-righteous.

INSIGNIFICANT ACADEMIC VS. LESS SIGNIFICANT ACADEMIC RIVAL

I certainly don't want to seem anti-education, all you professors out there. I am sure that it's extremely important to the starving children of Africa that you just discovered heretofore unrecognized patterns in the prefixes of their clicking language.

NAKED MOLE RAT VS. MOLE RAT IN FORMAL WEAR

The Naked Mole Rat leads my list of animals I would not like to be resurrected as. The list: 3. Lobster. 2. Cockroach. 1. Naked Mole Rat. Animals I would like to be resurrected as: 3. Bear. 2. Ape. 1. Centaur. (The last is a long shot, but I'm holding out hope.)

HAN SOLO VS. INDIANA JONES

Harrison Ford had a run there in the early '80s. Has anyone been cooler in movies ever than he was from 1980 to '82, when he was Han Solo, Indiana Jones, and Rick Deckard all in a row? Come on, it's a legit question—Nicholson tore it apart in *Chinatown* and *One Flew Over the Cuckoo's Nest,* but those were antihero roles, guys with flaws, more about acting and less about kicking ass. Same with Pacino when he did *Godfather II* and *Dog Day Afternoon* back-to-back. Newman had *Cool Hand Luke* and *Butch Cassidy and the Sundance Kid,* but *Butch Cassidy and the Sundance Kid* sucked, and "Raindrops Keep Falling on My Head" is not a hero's theme song. Really, it's Ford's 1980–82 against Eastwood's 1964–66 Spaghetti Western trilogy against Bogart's 1941–42 *(The Maltese Falcon, Casablanca).* I might have to go with Ford, but I could definitely argue about this endlessly on the Internet.

SMALL MAN WITH BREASTS VS. LARGE BALDING WOMAN

I think this is a question that everyone, at some point in their lives, has asked themselves.

BILL AND TED VS. MARTY McFLY AND DOC

When we finally do travel through time (and my scientific understanding is that's happening on Tuesday), will we do so with ignorance or erudition? Will we be really short but very cool, or will we be kind of tall and give the worst performance of all time in *Dracula,* which was a shitty-ass movie to begin with? Will Crispin Glover exist in our past, and will he be just as weird then as he is now? Can we go back to when George Carlin was really fucking funny, and not just an old man with observations? (Note on time travel: If I may make two requests—First: Late 1978, backstage at CBGB, Debbie Harry on my lap, I'll take it from there. Oh, and I'm, like, my age now, not three years old. Two: Late 1993, the big bungalow facing the pool at the Chateau Marmont with Winona Ryder. It's cool if I'm eighteen. I was thinner and still had hair.)

JUDAS VS. BENEDICT ARNOLD

Nothing's worse than betraying a brother. Look at the Mafia—the guy who bashes a guy's head in, everybody's cool with. The guy who snitches on the guy who bashes a guy's head in, *that's* the asshole.

DAVID DUKE VS. DAISY DUKE

The major advantage Daisy has here, besides the jean shorts, is the Waylon Jennings theme song. What's the Klan's theme song, and who sings it? Maybe if the Klan had a really catchy theme song the whole White Power movement would gain some steam.

PLATO VS. PLUTO

A battle between man's higher abilities and his animal instincts, as exemplified by a lovable cartoon dog. Of course we want to chase our tails; we must. But should we not think of what the ideal form of tail-chasing is, and what sort of society best supports it?

HOBBITS VS. THE SEVEN DWARFS VS. SMURFS

Little people can be tough. They've got a chip on their shoulders, and they'll punch you in the nuts just as soon as look at you. Though all of these mites are sure enough adorable (well, the Hobbits' hairy feet are a bit gross), that doesn't mean they should be taken for granted, as they all have very large responsibilities, which they handle with fierceness and aplomb. But that should hardly surprise us. Little people also make our world go around. I'm speaking, of course, of Third World sweatshop workers.

MAD COW VS. SAD COW

I believe the conversation went something like this in Britain sometime in the 1980s: "I have a thought, Alistair. Let's feed cows the ground-up remains of their own species." "That's a jolly good idea, Basil. I shall begin the cow cannibalization process the instant I finish dining on my recently deceased sister."

PEE-WEE HERMAN VS. GEORGE MICHAEL

This is included because I felt the book was embarrassingly light on masturbation references. It's well-known in literary circles that you can never have too many beat-off jokes; I believe Franz Kafka said that. Still, I had to hold back some material for my upcoming *Encyclopedia of Masturbation.*

CAP'N CRUNCH VS. TONY THE TIGER

Breakfast cereal characters are like blank canvases for the paintbrush of the young mind. Sure, Lucky the Leprechaun loves his Lucky Charms, but why? What's his motivation? His backstory? Of course Tony the Tiger thinks Frosted Flakes are grrreat, but what is he hiding? No one can be that excited about cereal without *something* else going on. The elementary-school breakfast cereal debates had two tiers. The first tier was which cereal tasted the best. This was one I couldn't participate in, as I wasn't allowed sugary cereals, a fact that made me build up great resentment and animosity toward my parents, which I still harbor to this day. Certainly, Cheerios and Grape Nuts weren't winning any fucking arguments. The second tier of the debate revolved around the personalities of each spokescartoon, and which one would win in a fight. I may have been a little bitter about Kix being my "treat" cereal, and I tried to convince my classmates that none of them—not the Trix Rabbit, the Cocoa Puffs Cuckoo, Lucky, Tony, the Cap'n—would fare well in a battle, as they were all hopeless doomed junkies. This is a position I still hold.

BOO BERRY VS. FRANKEN BERRY

I swear my parents didn't let me have one goddamned cocoa puff. You know what I would have done for a honey smack? Actually smacked a kid, until I either got a bowl of the cereal or got sent to juvee. I was serious, man. I'm sorry. Bad memories. Oh, sociocultural significance? Please see Cap'n Crunch vs. Tony the Tiger for a discussion of the importance of breakfast cereal characters. Also, while Franken Berry is a freaky monster, Boo Berry is a ghost. And the question of how a ghost would do in a fight is of *critical* importance. You can't hit them, presumably. But they can't hit you either. If the ghost is like Patrick Swayze he can move objects, which would make him a favorite against any human since, being dead, he also has little to lose. But object-moving does not seem to be a skill of every ghost. I can look that up, though.

TICKLE ME ELMO VS. FUCK ME DOLL

Your little boy's all grown up now, and you might want to think twice about entering his room without knocking.

HYPOCHONDRIAC VS. LEPER

Some people have real problems.

ROCKY VS. RAMBO

Stop, Sylvester. Just stop. We get it—you're more ripped than 99 percent of guys half your age. Amazing. Wow, you just kicked ass again. Remember when you used to act? Play a crotchety old father or something, or a disillusioned old cop who's seen his best years. Wait, you did that in *Copland*, and you were good. You know who wrote and starred in *Rocky*, a film that won Best Picture? Yes, that was really you.

THOMAS EDISON VS. MacGYVER

If I had been either of these guys, I would have stayed home and worked on a blow job machine. True, you don't get to change the world or save lives, but it's so worth it.

GANDALF VS. OBI-WAN KENOBI

I never much wanted to be a wizard: It seemed to me a step beneath superhero, and a bit too much like a Vegas magician. (With all apologies to Criss Angel. Love it when you levitate, guy.) Admittedly, this was a bit of an ego issue; a wizard tends to be the man *behind* the man, telling him the nature of the One True Ring or The Force. As an "adult," I understand what that's about—myths are often better if the guy burdened with the responsibility to save the world is average, relatable, Mark Hamill-ish, rather than a guy with a white beard and an assortment of parlor tricks. Plus, despite their spells and knowledge, when wizards do fight their record's not great. Gandalf the Grey "dies" on the peak of Zirakzigil from battling the Balrog, and Obi-Wan bites it against Darth Vader. Hey, but then they magically reappear, powerful as ever! Gandalf the Grey becomes Gandalf the White and Obi-

Wan becomes one with The Force, like coming back from the dead is just another magic trick. Lame. This battle, the wizards come off the sidelines and onto the field. Wizard-on-Wizard action, no resurrections allowed.

INSOMNIAC VS. NARCOLEPTIC

Who are these people who work all day, barely sleep at night, and then exercise for an hour at the crack of dawn? If I don't get a good seven, eight hours of shut-eye, I swear to God, I'll smack a baby just for whining. Go right up to someone's baby and punch it in the head for wanting its "ba ba." The good thing about that is, not only is it wonderfully cathartic, but abusing an infant really gets my adrenaline going and wakes me right up.

PASSION FRUIT VS. SIT AT HOME AND MASTURBATE FRUIT

Life is not always so succulent.

VOLTAIRE VS. VOLTRON

At first I thought this battle was simply about the manifestation of the boy's childhood impulses versus the manifestation of man's adult academic thought—a sort of Blake-esque confrontation of innocence and experience. Nay, it is so much more than that. Voltaire vs. Voltron asks whether the lights of Enlightenment will grow too bright and hot, and burn us like lasers from a giant mecha-robot. Will humanity, in a tragic act of hubris, fly too close to the searing heat of our own minds, and be, as Auden describes Breughel's Icarus, *the white legs disappearing into the green water*? Do we know just enough to destroy ourselves and not enough to be saved? I felt *The Official Compendium of Imaginary Fights* was worth writing only if I asked these sort of questions, the difficult and important questions. Questions like Voltaire vs. Voltron may ultimately determine the survival of our species. I am only one man, but I aim to be a superhero of the imagination, swooping down to catch a boy falling from the sky the moment before he is swallowed up by the sea. Read this tome carefully, friends, and heed its words of wisdom. This book can save the world.

ACKNOWLEDGMENTS

Many thanks to Chris Frost, a great friend and better illustrator. Two bear-sized thank-yous to Matthew Elblonk and Adam Korn, whose guidance and support made this book happen. Much gratitude to all the experts and all their expertise. And tyvm to Justin "Monkey" Sullivan, Dan "Little Monkey" Tepper, John Frost, Jaime Meline, and Jon Zachary for contributing to the goofiness—in this book and beyond.

ABOUT THE AUTHOR

Jake Kalish is a freelance journalist and humorist whose work has appeared in *Details, Maxim, Stuff, New York Press, Spin, Blender, Men's Fitness, Poets and Writers,* and *Playboy,* among other publications. He could totally kick your ass.